JACKS, JOBBERS AND KINGS

JACKS, JOBBERS AND KINGS

Logging the Adirondacks
1850 - 1950

by

PETER C. WELSH

NORTH COUNTRY BOOKS, INC.
Utica, New York

JACKS, JOBBERS AND KINGS
Logging the Adirondacks
1850 - 1950

ISBN 0-925168-30-0

Library of Congress Cataloging-in-Publication Data

Welsh, Peter C.
   Jacks, jobbers, and kings : logging the Adirondacks,
1850-1950 / by Peter C. Welsh.
      p. cm.
   Index
   ISBN 0-925168-30-0
   1. Logging—New York (State)—Adirondack Mountains
Region—History. 2. Loggers—New York (State)—Adirondack
Mountains Region—History. I. Title.
SD538.2.N7W45 1995
634.9'8'097475—dc20   94-9095
                                                        CIP
                                                        REV.

Cover: *Woodsman No. 1* by Amy Jones (1899-1992)
Courtesy of The Adirondack Museum

Frontispiece: *Autumn Morning, Racquette Lake* by A. F. Tait
Courtesy of The Adirondack Museum

Endpapers: *Lumbering 1908* by Seth Moulton
Courtesy of The Adirondack Museum

NORTH COUNTRY BOOKS, INC.
PUBLISHER—DISTRIBUTOR
311 Turner Street
Utica, New York 13501

For Jamie

"I want you to slow up at several points after leaving North Creek and Indian Lake and Blue Mountain Lake and Long Lake . . . where you will see some beautiful mountain scenery and enough virgin timber to make you want to stop to build a sawmill. . . ."

—*W. L. Sykes*, 1936

Contents

Foreword and Acknowledgments.. vii

Chapter One
Men and Machines in the Forest.. 1

Chapter Two
Emigrés from Pennsylvania 33

Chapter Three
Diversity Among the Pines.. 66

Chapter Four
The Realities of Utopia... 86

Chapter Five
The Hazards of Woods Work.. 103

Chapter Six
The Woods Ablaze 128

Chapter Seven
Conservative Forestry: An Epilogue 149

Endnotes 179

Index 187

Foreword and Acknowledgments

This book describes the process of logging the Adirondacks, a discrete area of six million acres, and how practices changed between 1850 and 1950. In one hundred years, logging went from a seasonal, labor-intensive, muscle- and animal-powered job to a year-round, machine-driven activity done by fewer workers armed with chain saws, skidders and motor-driven vehicles. It is also the story of an industry which changed from one characterized by total laissez-faire practices to one of tight and restrictive governmental regulation.

The book's origin was a monograph from which an exhibition was planned and installed at the Adirondack Museum in Blue Mountain Lake, New York that depicts the history of logging in the mountains. The manuscript's evolution into something more than a research report was prompted by a resource housed at the museum: 272 manuscript boxes containing the records of the Emporium Forestry Company and the Grasse River Railroad of Conifer, New York. It was a company founded by W. L. Sykes (1859-1941) that operated in the Adirondacks during the first half of the twentieth century. The company's records fortuitously survived the company's demise, and were brought to the museum in the 1970s by the museum's librarian Marcia Smith (who has since passed away). Without this source the book would not have taken the form it has: a study that has benefitted from some personal recollections and oral history, but is mostly based on the business records of the Emporium Forestry Company and its Pennsylvania parent, the Emporium Lumber Company. Between access to the Emporium records and research of contemporary media published at the heyday of Adirondack lumbering, the work became an old-fashioned documentary history of the subject rather than a reminiscence.

Beyond the perspicacity of Ms. Smith has been the author's most valued friendship with W. L. Sykes' two granddaughters and their husbands: Jean Sykes LeCompte and Philip; and Virginia Sykes Dreby and Edwin. Jean, the daughter of George W. Sykes (1886-1965), and Virginia, the daughter of W. Clyde Sykes (1887-1969), have been generous beyond belief in providing memorabilia, records, photographs and conversation that have helped in understanding the family history and the business of logging. Because of them, W. L. Sykes and his two sons—the principals of Emporium seem real, and the hardship of logging the northwoods more understandable. I am also indebted to George Sykes of Thomaston, Maine, Jean's brother, who has been an additional source of information.

Pictures of early logging abound in photographic collections, more so than in other media. The Adirondack Museum's Historic Photograph Collection provided outstanding views of the rigors and often brutal conditions under which the woods worker labored. The generosity of the museum in permitting the use in this book of these valuable windows to the past is greatly appreciated. So, too, was the kindness of John Stock who shared many of his photographs and slides, particularly those included herein. Few persons can match John's encyclopedic knowledge of all things pertaining to the woods.

My knowledge of the terrain, both social and physical, of the villages of Conifer and Cranberry Lake and the Emporium enterprise was widened by time spent with Tony Gensel of Tupper Lake. Tony, who was born in Conifer of parents who had come to the Adirondacks with the Sykes from Pennsylvania, generously toured the author over the Forestry Company's landscape and helped him to "see the forest for the trees." It was an experience surpassed only by traversing the sixteen mile right-of-way of the Grasse River Railroad with Jean Sykes LeCompte as my guide. Both adventures were rare treats. In a slightly different way, I am indebted to John Demer and the Harper's Ferry Center of the National Park Service. The invitation to speak there in 1987 on the subject of logging in the Adirondacks was enormously helpful in focusing the direction the book took and my attempt to portray the northwoods logging experience within the context of a special sense of place.

Most projects, particularly writing ones, usually have some basis in past experience, and often are fueled by coincidences found between the author and subject. In this case, I too had come to New York from Pennsylvania, and had a prior logging life in Potter County as had the Sykes family. My experience had not been as a lumber baron or 'jack, but rather as a person whose duties, among many, included general oversight of the Pennsylvania Lumber Museum near Galeton, the home base of W. L. Sykes and his family prior to their coming to the Adirondacks in this century's early years. It was at this museum, under the tutelage of its curator, Dolores Buchsen, that I learned about the hemlock forests, log loaders, sawmills, bunkhouses and mess halls that typified the industry. Thus my trip from Galeton to Conifer, from Potter County to St. Lawrence County, and from processing the hemlock of Pennsylvania's northern tier to harvesting hardwood in northern New York was far shorter in time and space than otherwise would have been possible. It was also a shortcut in learning about and understanding the character and strength of the men and women who worked the woods in a cruel and dangerous environment. My work, unlike the lumberjacks, was made all that much easier by knowing Potter County first.

I am indebted to a number of other persons, among them the staff, past and present, at the Adirondack Museum: Paul Bourcier, Hallie Bond, Tracy Meehan, Jim Meehan and Jerry Pepper. To others who read the manuscript and offered critical comments and suggestions—particularly David Salay, Warder Cadbury, Edward Comstock, Jean and Philip LeCompte and Jane Welsh—go my sincere appreciation. The book is infinitely better for their contributions. No less valuable, however, has been the skillful editing and preparation of the manuscript by Jane Mackintosh. She made what otherwise would have been an impossible task for the author a painless and creative experience which has enhanced whatever value the book might have.

Finally, no woods-job ever got done well without a good woods-boss and in the case of this book it, too, would not have gotten done without the unceasing effort of my wife and faithful colleague, Caroline. In every sense, *Jacks, Jobbers and Kings: Logging the Adirondacks 1850-1950* is as much her book as it is mine. It would never have been completed without her gentle prodding, insightful perceptions and high sense of professionalism.

—Peter C. Welsh
Tupper Lake, New York
1995

"The Choppers" *by Seneca Ray Stoddard, c. 1898.*

CHAPTER ONE

Men and Machines
in the Forest

"Thousands of men are seen entering into the dark
depths of the great woods."
                                    —*Harper's Weekly*, 1892

"The typical operation now consists of six men
who daily commute to the woods, two skidding
tractors and two trailer trucks."
                                    Northeastern Logger, 1963

Lumbering in New York was for many years one of the state's primary industries. In the North Country alone it flourished in such towns as Tupper Lake, Newcomb, Conifer, Lyons Falls, Poland, Watertown, Carthage, Potsdam, Glens Falls, Fulton, Hudson Falls and many more. Some of these towns sprang up quickly, as did early mining towns out West. As late as the 1950s many Adirondack towns still depended on turning wood into useful products, and many outlying villages had become bona fide cities, but most had had their heyday. This book is a story of one hundred years of logging in the Adirondacks as seen through the men and companies who did it. It is a history of men, machines and the changes which transformed the lumberjack from a man with an axe, crosscut saw and a horse to an industrial worker wearing a hard hat, armed with an array of machinery.

In 1850, the Empire State ranked number one in the nation in timber cut, but its output of sawlogs declined steadily after that in comparison with the rest of the country. New York led the nation again in 1912 with the production of pulpwood. The industry slumped in the Depression years of the 1930s as the supply of timber dwindled. The major part of the lumber industry moved west to the Lake States and the Pacific Northwest, and south to the pine-rich regions of the Carolinas, the timbered slopes of West Virginia and the southern Appalachians. Lumbering in the Adirondacks was temporarily revitalized by a surge of salvage operations following the great "blow down" or hurricane of November 25, 1950, which damaged over half a million acres of Adirondack forests. Lumbering still continues though on a much different scale than early in this century when it was a pervasive way of life.

In the nineteenth century, logging was a highly labor intensive operation, but in the early twentieth century major changes occurred in the industry. Gradually, power-driven machinery began to replace men and horses as the principal means of harvesting. Mechanization—chain saws for cutting, tractors for skidding, trucks for hauling—changed logging from a seasonal occupation into a year-round one. Today the entire lumber industry has become highly developed and technical, manned by skilled workmen operating complex machinery.

Logging operations began on the fringes of the Adirondack region as the nineteenth century opened, and worked their way into the heart of the wilderness by 1850. By then, the techniques of logging had become fairly standardized: it was an occupation marked by arduous physical exertion with tools little changed from medieval times—felling axes and hand saws—with men and animals providing most of the power. The longest phase of its history was eotechnic in character. In other words, in terms of power applied and materials used, it was a complex of wood, water and muscle power that characterized logging at least to 1850 and in many instances well beyond. When the steam engine, both stationary and locomotive, entered the woods—as it did *en masse* after 1850—logging began slowly to demonstrate the paleotechnic characteristics of a coal-powered and iron-structured environment or complex.

Only after the 1920s did the industry and the mountain society it supported evolve into a neotechnic phase where electrical power drove the machines of wood production and where materials used in the workplace and at home became alloys. This meant electric lights, electrically driven sawmills and ever-lighter chain saws; in the home it was pyrex, aluminum cookware and electric ovens instead of iron pots and woodstoves. In the villages and the woods it was the automobile. Finally then, in the Adirondacks, a paleotechnic phase of society had come to pass, if not altogether a neotechnic one.

Severe climate and difficult terrain made logging mostly a seasonal occupation in the region until the late 1920s and early 1930s. Cutting, barking, and skidding were done in the late summer and early autumn; loading, hauling and banking were done in the winter; driving began in the spring when the lakes and rivers were high from the spring thaw and run-off. In 1905, the journal *New York Lumber* explained how the weather set everything in motion.

> "Now that the logging country is plentifully supplied with snow as a result of the storms of the past week, teams and camp supplies are being rushed to the woods and lumbering operations will be well under way with the opening of another week. The opening of the season has been considerably delayed by lack of snow, but it is now believed that no further delay will be experienced. Choppers will follow the teams and camp supplies later in the week and hundreds of them will find employment in the lumber camps until spring."[1]

The men who logged the woods worked hard and labor turnover was high. In 1952, *The Lumber Camp News* reminisced that "a jobber had three gangs at the same time: One coming, one staying and one going," and their purpose was to cut trees, move them to the banking grounds and prepare to drive them to market.

Harper's Weekly, in 1892, published an article entitled "Busy Times in the Adirondacks" which told its readers that "the real stir . . . begins with the first snowfall. About this time there is a great demand for choppers and loggers." The snows brought out "all sorts of conditions of men—Canadians, Green Mountain boys, Yankees, etc.," and, in the space of several weeks, "thousands of men are seen entering into the dark depths of the great woods."

Snow was an important ally of the logger. In 1912, Professor Austin Cary from the University of Minnesota wrote to the Emporium Forestry Company at Conifer asking how snow helped the lumbering process. W. Clyde Sykes, a member of the family which owned and operated the company, replied that it "may be said to help . . . by furnishing a reliable season of some length in which hauling may be done." He went on to explain that this was particularly true "in the Adirondacks as we always have snow to depend on. . . . However, in Pennsylvania and western New York we find that the season is much shorter and it is a poor policy to depend on snow to do very much work."

"The headquarters of the Adirondack Lumbermen," wrote Lee J.

Vance, a frequent contributor to late-century popular journals, "are in camps far up in the mountains near the headwaters of the Hudson River, and miles away from any settlement." Writing for *Godey's Magazine*, Vance in 1896, cast a romantic cloak over everything. Felling, he explained, began "in the dim daylight" outside, in a "nipping and an eager air." The men were divided into gangs of tens or twenties; one gang did the chopping, another the skidding and hauling of logs.

> "An industrious chopper will cut from fifty to sixty logs a day, while expert axemen under favorable conditions have cut one hundred logs in a day. The number of logs cut makes some difference in the pay, where the choppers are paid according to their industry. Thus the rate of lumbermen's wages ranges from $25 to $40 per month, and board."[2]

In the 1890s, the logger had little in the way of power-driven equipment to assist him at any stage of his operation save low pressure steam engines (cumbersome and unwieldy) and the evolution of iced-roads. There simply was very little improvement until the introduction of the internal combustion engine. The order of business continued to be fourteen-hour days working by torch and lantern light and a body full of tired and aching muscles. Mechanization eventually changed the more familiar face of logging. Nelson T. Samson wrote in 1952 that the entrance of the machine into the woods was

> "... one of the strongest forces tending to de-seasonalize woods work, which in turn, will attract more steady men into the woods industries. Road construction is now almost completely mechanized. More all-season roads in the woods will allow more men to live in town and commute to work. With the prospect of being able to live a normal family life, more married men will accept woods employment."[3]

The great changes occurring in logging were summarized in 1936 by J. D. Gilmour:

> "Science has produced the internal combustion engine, first gas then Diesel; new alloys of metal and methods of working them; electric power is now universal; mass-production methods have been developed to the nth degree. Diesel power units are now available both as stationary units, and as mobile units in the form of tractors. Tractors are available in various sizes, and are rugged and dependable."[4]

Again, according to Samson, the breakdown of seasonality "cuts the ties that bind workers to companies and weakens the possibilities for hospitalization in group insurance plans, paid vacations, retirement plans and the like." But at the same time, application of the machine to woods work "has tended to draw more skilled men into the woods. As a natural consequence the operation of power saws, loaders, trucks, tractors, and other mechanical equipment, normally requires a more highly skilled man. . . ." The result was that the lumberjack had to be able to keep the equipment operable, hence the need to attract those with mechanical skills beyond the use of just axe and saw.

The economic strictures of the seasonal aspect of the business were characterized by George W. Sykes in a letter to the First Citizens Bank & Trust Company of Utica on February 16, 1934.

> "Most hardwood operations in the Adirondacks have been conducted . . . from the time money would first begin to be put into cutting and skidding of logs in the fall . . . through hauling in the winter, and the sawing in the mill in the winter, spring, and summer. . . . The seasoning and time required to sell and collect the return was necessarily pretty long, sometimes as much as eighteen months or more for a considerable part of it from one fall until the second spring following."[5]

Two years later, W. L. Sykes wrote that "last winter we bought about one million feet of hardwood logs at Newcomb which is about ten miles east of Long Lake," and a good fifty miles from Conifer, Sykes' office and center of business. The transaction seemed straightforward until one learns that the logs "were hauled on trucks to our Conifer mill in the coldest winter weather when the snow was thirty inches deep."

When the jobber's contract called for hemlock tan bark, work had to start early in the summer since peeling was most easily done from mid-May to about mid-August when the sap flowed. The crews were divided and each person was given a particular task. The best axemen were assigned to cutting large hemlocks, others girdled the fallen tree trunks with their axes at about four foot intervals whereupon men with "spuds" peeled or, perhaps more accurately, pried the bark loose. The first ring was made at the base of the tree and bark taken off before the tree was felled so as not to spoil that section of bark. Another group known as swampers piled the bark prior to hauling. Interestingly, from about 1850 to the 1890s, the axe was the only tool used for cutting, particularly in the region around Blue Mountain Lake. According to Harold K. Hochschild in *Township 34*, published in 1952, it was not until about 1891 that the crosscut saw was first employed in this part of the woods by a couple of fellows remembered as "foreigners," probably

Scandinavians.

In the autumn when the sap stopped and the bark peeling was finished for the year, the axemen began to cut spruce, pine and balsam. The forest echoed with the sound of trees hitting the ground. Choppers set the tempo and pace for the entire job. The axemen were so skilled, according to legend, that they could drop a tree on a stake preset as a mark on the line of fall and drive it into the ground. Considerable skill was needed to avoid getting the cut trees lodged in the branches of trees nearby; also, as logging techniques became more enlightened, an effort was made to protect, as far as possible, young saplings in the surrounding area.

Building and preparing skidways proceeded along with felling. In the early days of logging, skidways were made of spruce or balsam, and often left in the woods to decay. By 1890, the increased market value of these wood-types for pulpwood caused woodsmen to use hardwoods for their skids. When softwood logs were used, they were cut up and taken away at the end of the season.

After felling, the logs had to be measured or scaled. The scaler took the diameter of each log within the bark at the smallest end and recorded it in his book. Finally, a man with a marking hammer stamped the log on both ends with the owner's mark. Scalers generally had a helper who assisted when large logs had to be measured at both ends. Before the days of mechanization, a good lumberjack skidded fifty logs a day.

As cutting and skidding progressed, the jobber detailed other crews to build roads from the skidways to the main road which in turn led to a lake or river bank where the logs were unloaded. If diagrammed, the log roads on a big job would look like a tree of life with its spreading branches. William Fox aptly pointed out: "The jobber must exercise no little engineering skill in selecting a line that will reach all the skidways, and at the same time preserve a practicable grade. It must be downhill all the way from the starting point, so that large loads can be hauled, and yet not so steep as to shove a team over the banks."

Fox observed that, in the northwoods, autumn arrives quickly. Jobbers always hoped for an early snowfall, because only then could the hauling begin from the skidways to the banking ground. With snow, the roads were scraped and smoothed and then sprinkled each night by a large horse-drawn water tank mounted on runners. This made a good ice surface, so good in fact that sand, sawdust, straw or brush had to be

Courtesy of The Adirondack Museum

"The real stir begins . . . with the first snowfall." —Harpers's Weekly, *1892.*

After felling, the logs had to be measured or scaled. Finally a man with a marking hammer stamped the logs on both ends with the owner's mark.

With snow, roads were scraped and smoothed and then sprinkled each night by a large horse-drawn water tank mounted on runners.

Large loads were driven by a teamster perched on the top log, ten feet or higher off the ground. A cord of peeled logs weighed nearly 3,000 pounds. There are 15 cords on this load.

364 logs, South Meadows, Lake Placid, New York, 1903. Left to right: Dudley, Henry Moody, Henry Kerr, Ed Kerr, driver.

thrown on the steep grades by "road monkeys" to slow the speed of the heavily loaded sleds. The banking or rolling ground was a scene of furious activity. Sleds drove up in quick succession, chains were unfastened and the huge piles of logs rolled off the sleds "with a bumping, thumping noise as the logs rebound from the frozen earth." He noted that on the way to the banking grounds, the teamsters vied with one another to see who carried the heaviest load. As the bunks on the sleds got larger, the horses got heavier. It was then possible to roll great pyramids of logs onto a sled at the skidway. The large loads were driven by a teamster who was perched on the top log often ten feet or higher off the ground. The largest loads were from five to six thousand board feet, but most were considerably less. Teamsters were expected to make a specified number of trips each day depending on the distance traversed—hauls varied anywhere from one to four miles. Teamsters were up before the rest of the crews, had breakfast, fed their teams, collected the running gear and were off and moving while, as romantically recorded, "the stars are still shining clear in the cold winter sky." They were the elite of the woods crews, being paid more and receiving wages for every day of the week whether they worked or not—because rain or shine, they had to tend their horses. The lumberjacks got paid for the actual days they worked, and for pieces cut. Fox concluded that, when weather curtailed cutting, there was no pay for a "jack" sitting in the bunkhouse. The jobber's work was done when he delivered his contracted number of logs to the banking grounds.

The Reverend C. W. Mason, one of the sky pilot missionaries to the lumber camps, recalled when he first visited the camps in the Adirondacks in 1915, that most of the work—skidding logs, breaking out log roads and hauling—was done with horses. Mason calculated that "a cord of peeled logs will weigh not far from three thousand pounds. A set of bobs, moved up with long, heavy hardwood bunks, will weigh well up towards a ton. If you build a load of five cords of logs you may figure for yourself about how much weight you have." Mason learned, "It is one thing to haul a load of five cords of logs on a downgrade, well iced road." It was an entirely different matter to haul that much weight four miles up a severe grade even with strong young horses that weighed about eighteen hundred pounds each.

Just before World War I, the Gould Paper Company of Lyons Falls had contracted with Murphy and Company to cut and move twenty-five thousand cords of pulpwood out of the Black River watershed in

Lewis County, western Adirondacks. This necessitated hauling loads up Ice Cave Mountain which lay between the Black River and the Moose— a grueling road if not an impossible one. By coincidence it was also in the same time period that Mr. Gould sent his woods superintendent J. B. Todd to meet with a man named Linn at Bagg's Hotel in Utica. Linn had a small manufactory at Morris, south of Utica, where he was producing track-type machines. He subsequently brought one of his tractors into the woods for a demonstration and the following morning "they hitched the tractor onto the load and started up the log road to the summit." Mason recalled that Linn and Todd

"... overtook one of Murphy's teams on the road hauling a load by short hitches. They yelled at the driver to get out of the road. He pulled off as far as he could and the tractor with the load pulled off the road the other way and they crowded past. Then they hitched a chain onto Murphy's load and hauled team and load back into the road, unhitched the chain and went on to the summit. There they left the load and came back for another, but the second trip they hauled up two loads, one behind the other. And the third trip they took three loads."

It wasn't long before

" ... the company built a garage large enough to hold ten or twelve tractors. . . . They heated the garage with steam and kept mechanics at work on the tractors through the night to have them ready for the next day's hauling. They also did all the breaking out of new roads with a five ton Holt Caterpillar. It was altogether a great relief for the horses."[6]

The horse was not yet obsolete, but the handwriting was on the wall. The tank had demonstrated its overland and overall terrain use in World War I. In the Adirondacks in 1919, logging concerns like the Emporium Forestry Company were corresponding with the War Department seeking information about the purchase of surplus, six-ton Renault tanks from which "the armor plate can be easily removed" and which "are suitable for tractors." The price was $3,000 each. Two months earlier, the Emporium people had written to the Holt Manufacturing Company, the makers of the Caterpillar. Their tractor was adapted for woods work on the West Coast in 1916 and perfected during the war years. The Emporium people told them that there was a splendid opportunity for Holt in the Adirondacks.

"There is a man here [Frank Sykes, W. L. Sykes's cousin] who is the inventor of a portable log slide that he has patented and introduced to such an extent that it is already in use on perhaps a dozen logging jobs in this vicinity as well as to some extent in adjoining states. This log slide not only reduces the cost of logging but also enables the contractor or 'jobbers' to work the year round instead of confining the movement of logs mostly to the winter months. However, we believe if a tracklaying tractor will work successfully in trailing logs in this type of slide, that another great forward step can be made in logging methods, for then horses would be used for skidding into the slide and making up trails only."[7]

In the 1920s and 1930s, despite the innovations of progressive company owners, it was clear that no matter how impressive the tractors and trucks were and might subsequently become, teams of horses could not be dispensed with for either skidding, short hauls or light toting. It was equally apparent, however, that the tractor would one day revolutionize logging methods particularly on long hauls and eliminate small stream driving with its attendant costs of stream renovation, manpower (drivers) and clean-ups. But as long as labor was relatively abundant and inexpensive, the full utilization and promise of machinery—particularly the tractor (Linns and more versatile models)—would remain unrealized in the Adirondacks.

It was not until the shortages of labor in the 1940s, because of the demands of World War II, and the demand for forest products during and following the war, that the use of tractors increased on logging jobs. Tractors were expensive pieces of equipment; in order to pay for themselves, they had to be kept in fairly constant use. This, in turn, meant increased rates of cutting on logging jobs. It also meant that work formerly done by teamsters and their horses now was done by machine operators. They were a new class of woods worker who were trained and skilled and therefore commanded a greater wage for their services. Despite increased cost, the tractor operated more steadily, did not need rest breaks, handled bigger loads, was cheaply stored and did not need to be fed when idle. Crawler-type tractors in the 1950s were usually preferred in places where the terrain was difficult; nevertheless, the heavy rubber-wheeled skidders slowly increased in popularity.

When tractors first appeared on saw-log jobs, there was little or no reaction to them in the form of technological conservatism or comment about the destruction they caused. However, when applied to pulpwood jobs, people worried. The increased power of the tractors for skidding heavier loads often caused serious damage to young trees; but, with proper training, care and supervision, operators soon learned that minimal destruction to young trees was insurance for their future. Once demonstrated the small tractors were fairly quickly accepted; in fact their use proved, despite initial equipment costs, that operating expenses were reduced all along the way thanks to "less road building, larger concentrations of wood, reduced loading costs, and best of all, no adverse effect on the management of the residual stand."

After the tractors came wheeled skidders. They scared forest managers half to death because no one believed they could be used in concert with good forestry practices. The fact was that they could. It merely meant even greater attentiveness on the part of owners and operators. They found

> " . . . that mechanized logging required complete pre-planning and layout before the job started. This was necessary because while supervision can keep ahead of a couple dozen horses with layout and inspection, try to get ahead of a dozen skidder crews once you are behind. Complete control is absolutely necessary if you want a good job done. The skidder crew is producing much more volume per day, therefore covers much more area; if not supervised closely, then much damage can be done before they are caught up with. This control is the forest manager's responsibility, therefore he must be prepared and willing to provide it to get a good job done."[8]

There was still conversation about "skidders versus horses" as late as 1981. Some of it was thoughtful and quite serious. The prevailing wisdom was that "it all boils down to the fact that horses certainly will make more of a resurgence in future years and they have application in special circumstances." But the overwhelming opinion contended that "they will never replace the skidders to any great degree. In fact the thought of horses trying to keep a 500,000-cord-a-year pulp mill supplied makes one shudder."[9] In reality, the horse had finally reached the end of its tether in the logging business, provided, of course, that gasoline and diesel oil remained a readily available fuel source.

The tractor was not the horse's only competition. There was the gasoline engine which had provided, by the 1930s, the horsepower of choice in transporting pulpwood directly from the woods to the mills and getting lumberjacks to the job sites. Old-timers recalled that "with the advent of the automobile, the buckboard vanished quickly in the

north woods." Always among the more innovative operators, Ferris J.
Meigs and his Santa Clara Lumber Company of Tupper Lake "was
among the first to utilize the automobile in its woods operations." The
Emporium Forestry Company's use of trucks was documented photographically in September 1918.

New technology had slowly replaced the total dependence upon
men's muscles and horses. The seasonal patterns of an industry were
changing through use of machinery that could overcome the elements.
It was apparent by the 1920s that even more efficient logging methods
could be tried. In many ways, the tractor was a symbol of the more
dramatic aspects of mechanization that eventually affected every stage of
the logging process.

In the earliest days, the woodsman ate his meals by a kerosene lamp,
cut down the forest with his hands, went to town in the spring, got
drunk as a lord and occasionally took a bath. But as the icing wagons
and horses and eventually the sleds disappeared, so did a way of life.
New patterns emerged. Robert C. Bethke pointed out in *Adironcack
Voices: Woodsmen and Woods Lore*, quoting retired lumberjack Ted
(Eddie) Ashlaw: "Nobody stayed in camp anymore." Not totally true,
nevertheless, a portent of the times. Ashlaw went on to say "everybody
stayed home and drove to it, because then they had their bulldozers, had
their roads right into camp where they could drive a car right in. That
made all the difference in the world. . . . Oh, hell, it weren't the same
anymore when they began to bulldoze those roads and drive cars right
to camp." Lumberjacks now returned home in the evenings. At work
they entered an "electrically-lighted, gasoline-powered, gas-heated world
complete with hot and cold running water." The logger and his men
became industrial workers. The hard hat had become a badge of class,
and the eight-hour day a measure of accomplishment.

At mid-twentieth century the change of method in Adirondack logging had been so complete, authorities generally agreed that "the standard gasoline-powered motortruck is now, and probably will continue
to be, the favorite tool for hauling timber products out of the northeastern woods." The uncertainty of road conditions was largely a thing of
the past and, more to the point, "the motortruck has been so improved
that it is now giving service that would have been thought impossible a
few years ago." In the 1950s, the only thing which precluded the use of
big diesel-powered trucks found in the western logging states was the

"many state and township roads in the wooded areas [that] are narrow and crooked, with bridges that will not carry heavy loads." As a result log-truck drivers were told that

" . . . the modern motortruck has been greatly improved in recent years. . . . Nevertheless, truck driving demands a high-type worker—sober, industrious, and alert. This is particularly true in logging work, where the truck driver must take heavy, bulky loads over a great variety of road surfaces, from rough-graded woods roads, through paved highways, to crowded city streets. He is on his own much of the time."[10]

Unquestionably change had occurred; in the Adirondacks, a lumber camp teamster of 1900 could not have imagined driving such a rig no matter how "sober, industrious and alert" he may have been.

In the spring of 1952, Finch-Pruyn was cutting pulpwood near Blue Mountain where "about 30,000 cords have been cut on the operation. The Blue Mountain tract is part of a much larger one owned by the company on the Hudson River and its tributaries, including the Boreas, the Cedar and Salmon River." Some of the cutting was being done on state land where the company was taking a large amount of timber which had resulted from the great blowdown of November 25, 1950. For years, Finch-Pruyn, through far-sighted management, had acquired large holdings within the Hudson River system that assured direct if not easy river driving to their Glens Falls pulp and paper mills on the eastern edge of the Adirondacks. Technological breakthroughs, however, were changing old patterns of transportation as well as lifestyles. For example, "with the more recent discovery that pulpwood fresh from the woods produced a superior grade of paper, plans were made to haul it directly from the woods to the mill by truck," saving the two-month to two-year delay that often came with river transport.

In the early history of the state, easy transportation of logs to market was confined to the natural course of rivers. Most of the lumber, after local needs had been met, was exported principally for the English market, the West Indies and the Wine Islands. Michaux, the French naturalist, in 1801 tells of white pine sawed at Skenesborough (Whitehall) then "transported 70 miles in the winter on sledges to Albany." All the lumber gathered along the Hudson was then "brought down in the spring to New York in sloops of 80 to 100 tons" to be transhipped "in great part to Europe, the West Indies, and the Southern States." This export trade had been active well before the days that river driving began.

The Lumber Camp News in May 1946 reminisced that if ever there was a spectacular aspect of logging, it was the river drive. It "began when the first spring freshets freed the river of its ice sheath and set in motion a harvest of logs." Tractors, and eventually trucks and railroads, eased and speeded the woodsman's work, but it was the drive that the old-timers remembered almost to a point of reverence.

For three-quarters of a century, the big mills at Glens Falls, Hudson Falls and Fort Edward were fed by the Hudson River which wends its way for eighty-some miles through the Adirondacks from the center of the region to the east and south. With dams being built to float logs out of the mountain streams which were otherwise too shallow, loggers could cut deep into the woods, away from the Hudson shoreline. Damming the streams was a widespread practice. "Only the best trees were felled," recalled L. E. Chittenden in 1893 in his *Personal Reminiscences*. "The logs were run down to the mills in the high water of spring." But it was not long until the lumbermen had a bright idea. "It was to dam the outlets—raise the water in the lakes so as to reach the pines upon their shores. The first dam was upon the Raquette River to raise the water in Big Tupper Lake. Dams at the outlet of Long Lake, Blue Mountain, Utowanna, Raquette, and many others speedily followed." The supply of timber was kept steady, and grew. In 1849, a sorting boom was built at Glens Falls by the Hudson River Boom Association. It reached its greatest capacity in 1872 with two million logs. This was the Big Boom remembered by many, lumbermen and villagers alike.

Log-driving was much more economical at the period than transporting large mills deep into the woods. Railroads soon altered this. The first railroad for logging purposes in the state was built in Steuben County in the mid-nineteenth century; Adirondack logging railroads quickly followed. By 1920, as the hardwoods became a staple of the lumber trade, railroad and truck transport annually increased in importance. As a consequence, there was a corresponding decrease in the number of river drives. By 1950, they were mostly a thing of the past.

The entire process of the river drive was described in 1886. When the logs came out of the woods, they could be seen

" . . . everywhere coming down, advancing endwise with the current. In many places of still-water the entire breadth of the river for some distance was closely covered with them. These were not so small as those usually seen in the main rivers, but were from full grown trees of the original forest spruce, from one to two feet in diameter. With the spruce logs were a few hemlocks, usually of larger size; a few pine logs, sometimes two or three feet in diameter, floated with the others. As the water was lowering, stranded logs were seen everywhere along the shore. They covered gravel banks and bars in the river, and were piled in disorder on the rocks of the rapids, or pushed over the water-falls stood on end in the midst of the white, pouring torrent."[11]

The chaotic aspect of the drive was deceiving. It had more system to it than was apparent at first glance. There was method and precision in the sorting of the logs of the different companies; the sawing, planing and dressing of the boards prior to sale and the shipment of finished lumber.

"When a full stock of logs is placed on the river, and the spring floods break up the ice and set the logs going, other contracts are made with the same or other men to drive the logs into the booms of the different mills at a stipulated price per log. If, as is usually the case, logs of several different companies are on the same river, all are driven down in common, and the drive is called a 'Union drive.' Arrived [sic] at the uppermost boom—formed by chaining together logs floating on the surface of the water and held in place by occasional piers, strong but rude structures of logs filled in with rocks, located above the first sawing station—the logs belonging to these mills are sorted out and turned into the different booms, while those belonging below are sent on their way down the channel."[12]

In 1892, *Harper's Weekly* told its readers that "the most difficult and dangerous part of the lumberman's work lies in sending thousands of logs to market. . . . The logs are rolled into creeks, which swell to rivers by spring freshets. A log may catch on a huge boulder, and at once it becomes the king pin of a 'jam.' " This is where things got tricky as "it is always a bold undertaking to free the imprisoned log." With the plug pulled, so to speak, "the jam breaks suddenly, and the drivers run for the banks." The obstruction which had built up a wall of logs behind it now became "a jumping, plunging, squirming mass." After a good bit of worry, work and no little amount of confusion,

" . . . logs from different parts of the Adirondacks come together at Schroon Lake. Then rafts of five and ten thousand pieces are made up, and are towed to the 'big boom,' which is an immense storage-place for the Hudson River lumbermen. . . . Those logs not selected by the saw and wood-pulp mills are sent on to Troy, Albany, and to New York, where there is a demand for spars, masts, and spiles."[13]

The drive was a good story for those who could not imagine such wild scenes in the course of their hum-drum, urban lives, as well as for those persons who never thought about where the wood for their houses, furniture or paper came from. It was such exciting stuff for the city-dweller that *Godey's Magazine*, in 1896, featured another illustrated article by Lee J. Vance that described the rigors of the river-drive with considerable flair. "The choppers," by April, "lay by their axes to become 'log-drivers' and now enter upon the most dangerous and exciting period of their continually adventurous lives. . . . For days and nights, and for weeks, they follow the logs on their journey" downstream.

Around the turn of the century, E. A. MacDonald of West Carthage in Jefferson County, recalled that, in sorting out logs, the night sorters were required "to sort 750 cords every night" in order to get everyone's logs properly separated. MacDonald's first-hand account corroborates the picture of the log drivers presented in the popular journals of the day only in a more folksy and personal way.

> "We worked from before 5 a.m. until 8 p.m., and $2.50 was top wages, with four meals a day. When it rained or snowed we would stand with our backs against a tree and sop up our beans, with snow flakes or rain water, being wet to our necks. It was so cold our teeth would chatter, so we hardly had to chew the food. Sometimes a lunch carrier would get lost, which was often the case. Then the men tending out would go eight and ten hours without anything to eat."[14]

Ferris J. Meigs, a transplanted Pennsylvanian and long-time president of the Santa Clara Lumber Company, recorded his recollections and impressions of the log drivers during their heyday.

> "Other lumber companies had their drives of logs in the Raquette River too, and great rivalry sprang up among the crews of the various logging companies. These rivalries often developed roughness and ill temper on the part of the driving crews—their purpose being to get one drive down the river ahead of the others, as the first flood waters made the driving less expensive. . . . When all is ready, the sluice gates of the upstream dam are opened and the logs above the dam are rushed through, and down the stream to the next dam. Along the stream at points where rocks or eddies or other conditions would likely catch

and hold the logs, wing dams were built so that the logs would run free. Men were posted along the stream to keep the logs running in the current. Often, too often, though all reasonable precautions had been taken, logs would form 'jams,'—logs piling up behind a few that had been stuck on some rock, often deep in the stream. A 'log jam' must be broken up at once.

Experienced 'drivers' usually would be able to find and pull out the 'key' log and the jam would break up. The men working on the jam in the middle of the stream would scramble for shore. A sure eye, experience, and agility were needed to prevent a tragedy. Occasionally, the 'key log' could not be found, and then dynamite was used. Several sticks lashed to a long pole, and with the waterproof fuse lit, were thrust as deep as possible into the front of the jam, and the explosion would tear away and loosen the jam."

And, as others have described:

". . . then the logs would come with a roar, pushed by the mass of water that had been gathering behind the jam. On a cold, frosty morning, it was an odd sight to see the workman in charge of the dynamite, thawing the cartridges around a fire; then with his long pole lashed to the half dozen sticks of dynamite rush across the jam to the middle of the stream, push the charge as deep as possible into the mass, then run to safety, and watch the logs tossed high into the air by the explosion. The crew were all alert to keep the logs moving once the jam was broken."

The drive must have been an exciting prospect at all stages, and you can more or less sense Meigs' relief when he said:

"Finally, the logs were in a solid mass above the 'sorting' works. During the long drive, logs belonging to other lumbering outfits, coming into the river from other streams, had become mixed up with the company's. Each log bore the registered brand of the various companies, stamped with a hammer on its ends, and at the 'sorting works' were distributed into their several booms—some for the local mills, and some for 'down river.' The 'sorting' was going on night and day, and the flaring torches on the sorting raft and the busy men, the workers and the watchers, made an interesting sight in the chill and quiet of the spring nights."[15]

With a good flow of water in the stream, a log traveled about two miles an hour. Seasonal conditions, the cost of labor and the volume of logs were variables that determined driving costs. Harold K. Hochschild in *Township 34* states that in the last decades of the nineteenth century, sawn logs could be driven from the Indian River, a tributary of the Hudson in Hamilton County, to the Big Boom at a cost of about ten cents per thousand board feet or about two cents a log. By the last years of the river drives, the cost had risen to about three dollars per thousand board feet.

The drive constituted "hazardous duty." The nineteenth century reminiscence of an old-time lumberjack captured some of the breathtaking moments and dangers involved.

> "If the river was good and it stayed good, you could put a log in at Newcomb and it would show up at the Big Boom in a matter of only two days. But with 13-foot logs, there was always trouble somewhere. The Boreas was bad all the way down. The Hudson was bad at Ord Falls, below Newcomb, bad again just above the mouth of the Indian, and very bad on the big bend below Blue Ledge, near the Deer Den. Even if the drive got through those spots, it could always hang up on the Moulton Bars at Warrensburg. The worst, though, was always that stretch past the Deer Den. That was where Russ Carpenter smashed up his bateau and disappeared under a boiling mass of logs. Months later some children found him 30 miles downstream when they saw a piece of red cloth sticking up through the gravel near Stony Creek. It was Carpenter's handkerchief, still tied around his neck."[16]

It took a special person, according to Hochschild, to face such risks. He had to know his business, have the confidence of his colleagues, and possess an extraordinary degree of athletic ability and strength. This was dangerous work, particularly for the jamboat crews. "In some instances the boat crews resorted to a charge of dynamite but, more often, they relied on their brawn and dexterity."

The drives were always big news in logging circles in the Adirondacks. Those on the Hudson fed logs out to the southeast, on the Moose out to the southwest, and on the Raquette to the northern boundaries of the region. Each season from 1939 until the 1950s, *The Lumber Camp News* and other publications faithfully reported them. The weather was perfect in 1939. "Melting snows had kept streams at fairly high levels throughout the region" for a substantial period of time. The crews of the Gould Paper Company led by Hugh Dowling had already gotten their logs past the camp at Moose River and were nearly finished for the season. A shorter drive, run by Elmer Bernier on Fish Creek had rapidly moved large quantities of wood to the jack works for trucking. On the

Cedar River, Thomas Arsenault and his men had driven 13,000 cords to the mouth of the river from whence it was driven down the Hudson to Glens Falls and the mills of Finch-Pruyn and Company. All of this was under the watchful eye of John Donahue, the company's driving superintendent. On Bureau Ponds, Donahue and Arsenault had used dynamite to break the ice and get the wood started down the Boreas to the Hudson.

The following year (1940) the reports of the drive were good except that in the interval John Donahue had died. He was replaced by William Smith as Finch-Pruyn's driving superintendent. Thomas and Arthur Arsenault were his driving foremen. The company intended to

> " . . . drive 32,000 cords in four-foot lengths on Beaver Brook and the Boreas and Cedar Rivers. This wood is driven down these three tributaries into the Hudson River and on the Hudson to the mill at Glens Falls. Ordinarily it takes about two months to drive this wood from the landings to Glens Falls mill. Some years ago, when the pulpwood was driven in the form of unpeeled logs, the logs would not reach their destination for at least two years. Then the four-foot grinders were installed in the mill and since that time, the wood has been peeled and cut into four-foot lengths in the woods. Transportation in this form is much easier on the small streams."[17]

At the Gould Company, some sixty men worked on the log drive. What was at times a capricious undertaking was described in May 1940, as a very orderly, systematic and routine movement of raw materials with twenty-two thousand cords of wood being driven down the Moose River. The rigors and hazards of an earlier time now seemed commonplace. It was reported:

> "Comparatively few men have been working in the vanguard of the logs, and at various points along the river. Most of them comprised the 'cleanup crew' who worked in boats and from shore as a sort of 'rear guard' to make sure that every last log reaches its destination at Lyons Falls. These men comb the banks, free minor log jams and get all of the timber that might have been delayed in its downstream journey moving again."[18]

It was one of the biggest log drives in over a decade and the reporter's description became less prosaic. He finally warmed to the real nature of the scene. It was a sight that pitted man against nature; one that was seldom matched by any other American pre-industrial enterprise, except whaling.

"Thousands upon thousands of logs have been floating down the Moose River during the past several days. . . . They have been coming from the camps of the Gould Paper Company and are floating through McKeever to the company's plant at Lyons Falls, a distance of some 50 miles. As far as the eye could see, the Moose River was dotted with the smooth-moving logs—until a jam formed. Then the timber stopped its downriver journey. The logs piled up, one atop the other, stacking in hodge-podge fashion like gigantic jackstraws. Then it was up to the drivers, those skilled, nimble-footed woodsmen, to disentangle the pile that towered 30 to 40 feet above the surface of the water."[19]

In April of 1943, the Second World War was in full swing and in the mountains there were five river drives underway. Finch-Pruyn was driving pulpwood down the Hudson from its tributaries; Johnston and Son were moving pulpwood down the Jessup River to Indian Lake; Elmer Bernier and his men were working Jones Brook and West Canada Creek driving unbarked wood to Nobleboro above Poland, where it was debarked by a barking drum and then trucked to the pulp mill. The Gould Paper Company had its driving crew ready to go on the South Branch of the Moose River to move log-length wood from the Adirondack League property near Old Forge to the mill at Lyons Falls, and lastly, the St. Regis Paper Company was preparing to drive about 15,000 cords at Crooked Lake. "Several scores of men" were reported on the ready "with their sturdy river boats, pike poles and peavies" set to move saw logs and four-foot pulp-wood to the various mills in the North Country.

The *Tupper Lake Free Press* had compared the spring drives to the cattle round-ups of the West saying, " 'white water men' rode herd on the winter's crop of logs." The newspaper told its readers that

" . . . the waters of the Raquette River and the broad expanse of Raquette Pond carry no 'freight' beyond an occasional sportsman's boat this spring, but older Tupper residents recall when an agile lumberjack could have traveled almost across the lake over the bobbing carpet of logs which floated in thousands there, bound for the sawmills of this village and of lumber towns farther down the river. . . . It was a time when millions of feet came down the river each spring."

These were the halcyon days of Tupper Lake village and the days of the sorting boom,

" . . . a spidery network which sprawled across Raquette Pond, to cor-

Tractors began replacing horses in hauling logs to the banking grounds after 1915. This Linn Tractor, seen here on February 10, 1931, was owned and operated by the Oval Wood Dish Corporation of Tupper Lake, New York.

By 1950, track-laying tractors, then skidders had largely replaced the horse on big jobs.

The Log Skidder Near Charlie Pond, Adirondacks, N.Y., *1981, by Stephen Story.*

Ferris Meigs and his Santa Clara Lumber Company of Tupper Lake were among the first to use the motor truck in woods operations. The Emporium Forestry Company's use of trucks is documentd in this photograph dated September 20, 1918.

River drives were among the most spectacular aspects of the logging process in the Adirondacks. Log jam on the lower Raquette River near Sissonville c. 1925.

The chainsaw was a technological innovation specifically applied to logging. Advertisements began appearing in The Lumber Camp News *in the 1940s; this particular one is from May 1945.*

ral the logs cut by the different lumber companies. Each log bore a punch mark on the end, and the experts at the sorting gap could tell at a glance whether to shunt the log into a holding boom, for the Santa Clara or A. Sherman Lumber Co., or some other mill here, or send it on down the river. The punch marks on the butts of the logs were to the drivers what the brands on cattle were to the ranch men of the west. There was the 'X' mark of the Usher mills; the 'O-O' of the Potter Wood at Colton; the 'F' of the Raquette River Paper Co.; the square of the A. Sherman mills; the triangle of the old Norwood Manufacturing Co., and many others."[20]

The days of the great drives had come and mostly gone by the late 1940s. The mechanization of logging had made archaic many of logging's basic techniques and practices. Motor driven machinery had replaced the hand tools and muscle power of the early days. In the post-World War II era, the chain saw, the truck and specialized moving, lifting and hauling equipment completed the great technological change in the industry's methods of operation which had begun earlier with the introduction of the Linn and Lombard tractors. In May 1950, *The Lumber Camp News* ran as its headline "Log Driving Program at Low Ebb." It went on to say that "the log driving program in many parts of the Northeast is but a memory. . . ." Only Finch-Pruyn was still driving logs on Adirondack rivers in 1950. The fact was that the truck and driver had taken the place of the river-men.

The high excitement of the drive lived on even if its primary skill, the agility of men on floating logs, had been reduced to the scheduled events of loggers' field days. The memory of those men who worked "Sundays or weekdays, fair weather or foul," whose occupation was "full of peril" and where men were "lost every year" was hard to forget. Men who knew where it was safe to go were the men who survived. But according to an 1886 account by the Forest Commission, "sometimes the most careful men became mixed with the rolling logs or seized by the current of the waterfall and are swept away." In 1917, Aaron Maddox thought that the river drive was "the worst part of lumbering." Danger was great and lives were lost every spring. Throughout the long history of the drives one single aspect remains remarkable—the fact that so many men survived.

In 1951, as the century of river transport was ending, Simmons' *Logger's Handbook* designated the axe as still the most important of all the tools that the logger used. Time studies in the northwoods showed that the pulpwood cutter used his axe almost half of his working time; the saw log cutter used his about one-third. It was important that the woodsman have an axe that was well-suited to the work he was doing and in good cutting condition; most of all, it was important that he know how to use it. The axe was perfected in the United States in the 1830s at a time when, as Siegfried Giedion has written, the Americans were reshaping the design of most hand tools. The American felling axe was an object admired by all who saw it. Year after year, it won awards at international expositions.

Second only to the axe, the tool most used by the logger was the crosscut saw. The *Logger's Handbook* informed that a dozen or more standard patterns, lengths and weights were available. The one to choose for a given job depended partly on individual preference and partly on the size of the trees to be cut. For the heavier saw log timber, the straight-back model was usually preferred. The blade was stiffer, less likely to be damaged when the saw became pinched. For small timber and pulpwood the narrow sway-back model was best. The narrow blade permitted a wedge to be driven in behind the saw even in shallow cuts. In the far West, the sway-back pattern was used in felling big timber because the narrower blade caused less friction.

In the history of logging in the Adirondacks, the metamorphosis of saw-types was important to both loggers and the industry. The cross-cut saw was introduced around Blue Mountain Lake in the 1890s and went to the job site with the lumberman's axe. These were the standard tools for decades, eventually supplemented by the light and wieldy buck saw. In reducing trees into block lengths, the buck saw speeded the work of the sawyer but did not materially ease his task. *The Lumber Camp News* of May 1950, reported:

> "The old method of converting hardwood standing timber into four foot pulpwood with the use of axe, buck saw and crosscut saw, required a considerable amount of strenuous work in notching, felling, limbing and sawing. In addition, experience and skill are also necessary in filing saws, which is a trade in itself."

Frank Reed, writing in 1939, cited the popularity of the buck saw which "was formerly used in Maine, New Hampshire and parts of Canada, [and] has now penetrated the Adirondacks so thoroughly that one can see many of them in operation on every job." To use it effectively, the sawyer had to keep it sharply filed, "an evening occupation . . . in practically all of the camps." Many prospective young woodsmen did not know how to file saws and as a result sought work elsewhere. "Experienced woodsmen who have made their livelihood from this type of work . . . are forced to give up piecework production because of impaired vision, as good eyesight is highly essential in filing saws."[21]

In the 1940s, the buck saw was the principle tool used during the skidding season. Directly related to the buck saw was the bow saw, which in 1951 was extensively used by pulpwood cutters in the northeast and Canada. It was of Swedish origin and design,

> " . . . an improved model of the old-type buck saw with a better blade and a frame that holds the blade under greater tension. Here we a have an excellent crosscut saw for one-man use on timber less than ten inches in diameter. For wood ten inches or more in diameter, the standard crosscut is a better tool."

But the bow saw was not commonly used for cutting hardwoods. "For this kind of work a two-man crosscut is generally considered easier to use, although production per man-day could almost certainly be increased by adoption of the bow saw."[22]

While hand saw styles were changing, and their individual virtues being explored, another tool was on the horizon which would completely change the concept of hand work: the chain saw, which began showing up in the Adirondacks between 1942 and 1952. Unlike the steam engine, the motor truck or the tractor, the chain saw was a technological innovation specifically applied to logging, not just an adaptive technology for forest use. By 1952 the buck saw was in decline and the chain saw had "very largely supplanted it, although some buck saws are still in use, particularly in very steep country and in places where timber is sparse."

The Lumber Camp News, which began publication in Old Forge in 1939, first mentioned chain saws in September 1944, with the acknowledgment that some companies were now using the machines because of wartime manpower shortages. Nelson Brown documents that the first chain saw was used in 1930 by Eastman Gardner Company of Laurel, Massachusetts. At first, they were mostly used for cutting pulpwood bolts and not for felling; some indication of technological conservatism is hinted at in the statement that "mechanical logging . . . will never take the place of the 'buck saw' man."

Many observers thought that the chain saw was "the first piece of mechanical harvesting equipment to move into the woods that made itself felt." At first they were dubbed "timber-murderers" and "wood's-butchers," but it was not long before sportsmen were taking chain saws into the woods on overnight camping trips. It was this group that had originally protested most loudly of all against the chain saw's introduction as a logging tool. Writing in 1951, Fred Simmons had declared that "labor shortages in the woods have stimulated interest in power saws." There was almost no limit to the sizes, power-sources and configuration of these early saws. "Almost any contraption that offered a promise of getting timber out faster with less labor has been tried." This resulted in "some very promising devices that should make the work of the northeastern logger easier and more productive."

Circular saws and drag saws were tried but the chain saw was "the most promising development in the power-saw equipment field." There was no question that its use increased production.

> "The new method of converting trees into four foot pulpwood with the use of power chain saws not only increases the amount produced daily by each worker but also makes the task much easier. . . . Most of the men using chain saws, not only cut the logs into four foot lengths with the saws but also notch, cut trees and limb them after they have been felled."[23]

The chain saw had many advantages. It seemed safer than the axe on the basis of early use, since 50% of all woods accidents were axe-caused; further, it speeded the productivity and hence the earning power of the woods worker; finally, it required less skill to operate. In 1950, it was "safe to say that most of the pulpwood produced in the future will be by using the mechanical chain saws."[24]

When and where the first chain saws were used in the Adirondacks is not totally clear; however, *The Lumber Camp News* is an index to early manufacturers and preferred models. The earliest advertisement for a chain saw appeared in May 1945, placed by A. C. Lamb and Sons of Liverpool, near Syracuse. Lamb claimed: "We have been fortunate in selling over 50% of all chain saws in use in New York State." The saw was a two-man Disston with a Mercury gasoline engine.

The second chain saw advertisement appeared in October 1945 and was put in by Burrill Saw and Tool Works of Ilion. Like Lamb and Sons, Burrill was drumming the merits of the Disston which "will fell a

30-inch tree in 75 seconds. It is a lightweight, powerful saw driven by a 7 or 11 [horsepower] 2-cylinder gasoline engine which speeds the cutting of all kinds of timber." It was described as "easy to operate," one which "requires limited experience" to use. It was a tool which "reduces man-power requirements, speeds up cutting, saves time and money." What was not stated was that the saw weighed in excess of 130 pounds.

F. H. Hadley of Black River advertised in *The Lumber Camp News,* May 1946, that he was the authorized agent for the "Universal" one-man power chain saw in "Oswego, Jefferson, St. Lawrence, Franklin, Lewis, Herkimer, Hamilton, Essex and Clinton Counties." The Universal was "the Jeep of power chain saws." Prospective buyers were informed that "the efficiency and reliability of the two-man power chain saw has been thoroughly proven in the logging field. There has been a widespread demand for a lighter, lower-cost, One-Man Power Chain Saw. This need is now met by the new 'Universal' One-Man Power Chain Saw."

The "Mall" Chain Saw was the third type advertised. It was a 36-inch saw which weighed 82 pounds and was powered either by electricity, compressed air or gasoline. In August 1946, it was available through A. C. Lamb and Sons or from the Slade Tractor Company in Albany. It was, according to Slade, "used extensively by Lumbermen and Pulp-wood Cutters" to whom the company had "delivered hundreds of these light . . . saws in northern and eastern New York." Like Disston and the Universal, the Mall was "speeding up jobs and cutting cost in every locality." Slade had a number of representatives selling the Mall: Eugene Boyer at Tupper Lake; Gilbert Springs at Indian Lake; Gorman Broth-ers at AuSable Forks; and C.M. Broadwell at Morrisonville.

By 1947, A. C. Lamb ran a bold-faced, half-page advertisement stat-ing: "The West Coast Chain Saw is Here." It was the "Titan" billed as "first in the field—16 years of know how, More Logs—Less Effort." The same years Charles S. Wade of North Creek began advertising the "Precision," an 18-inch power-driven bow saw for cross-cutting pulp-wood. There were "over 3,000 Precision Power Chain Saws now in operation throughout Canada and the United States." But Disston still appeared to be the favorite model in the North Country. In 1948, Bur-rill Saw and Tool Works exclaimed: "Look! Here is what the pulpwood cutter has been waiting for. It is the new dependable Disston One-Man Chain Saw." It must have been good because these machines "took all of the chain saw prize money at the Woodsmen's Field Day Contest in Old Forge on July 17, 1948." Just a little less than a year later, Burrill opened a "Northern Service Branch at Bird's Boat Livery on Route 365 at Raquette Lake, New York."

In June 1949, the first of many advertisements appeared proclaiming the advantages of another version of the chain saw made by McCulloch Motors Corporation of Los Angeles. Three months later, *The Lumber Camp News* ran a full two-page spread asking, "What makes the McCullochs so easy to use?" and then gave ten reasons: they were easy to carry, operated in any position, swiveled 360 degrees, started quickly, cut fast, wouldn't stall, were suited to one- or two-man use, had convenient controls, and wasted no time in setting. The McCullochs were available in six different models, including one bow-style saw ranging from twenty inches to sixty inches and in price from $385 to $425, all f.o.b. Los Angeles. By November 1949, nine models were available and by January 1950, ten models were on the market with the least expensive now listed at $295. The Homelite Corporation of Port Chester took a full page in *The Lumber Camp News* announcing that its new one-man chain saw— "the one you've always wanted"—could be seen "in operation at Woodsmen's Field Day, Tupper Lake, N.Y., August 12 and 13, 1949."

Lastly, a decade after *The Lumber Camp News* was first published, an advertisement appeared for the Pioneer, "the First Manufacturers of Chain Saws in North America" and "the oldest, most experienced manufacturer of chain saws" in the United States. "Thousands . . . are in use throughout the Americas and in overseas countries under all kinds of cutting conditions." In the Adirondacks, too, the Pioneer was a well-used and popular saw. Pioneer's motto, "Built to Stay in the Woods," turned out to be the truth not only for the Pioneer but for chain saws in general. In the woods, after 1950, the man with the axe and crosscut saw was more likely to be a man with a chain saw supported by tractors, skidders and trucks. The machine was in the Adirondack forest to stay.

Ten years later Lyman A. Beeman, president of Finch-Pruyn, told a group of pensioners "that the company now purchases about 50 percent of its hardwood from local farmers and woodlot owners, while the other 50 percent comes from company woodlands in the Adirondack Mountains, harvested by independent loggers." He went on to say that "the company no longer maintains logging camps." The days of the large camps were over.

"The typical operation now consists of six men who daily commute to the woods, two skidding tractors, and two trailer trucks. Horsepower has replaced manpower wherever possible, and the woods echo with the chattering of the chain saw, the steady drone of the skidding tractors and the powerful snorts of the heavy trucks."[25]

Between 1950 and 1960 the modern logger (jobber or contractor) working a site efficiently had to have the following motor-driven logging equipment to compete successfully:

"Two HD-5 tractors, one having a bulldozer, and both having winches; two-man chain saws; a rubber-tire Carco logging arch; and a log loading derrick. Recently, they have changed to the use of one-man chain saws in the woods, and a two-man chain saw on the landing. Where the timber is somewhat scattered, it is felt that two one-man chain saws are more efficient. The one-man saw is also advantageous in that some production can be maintained even though one of the cutters misses a day."[26]

Logging was a business intended to make money. It was often big business where Adirondack lumber companies owned or controlled thousands of acres of choice forest lands. They maintained company towns, closely monitored the supply of raw material (logs, pulpwood, and bark), the means of production (men and mills) and sometimes built and operated their own logging railroads. They also, in most respects, set the standards—in production, in progress, and in quality of life for those whose lives were lived in the woods. W. L. Sykes and his Emporium Forestry Company were among the more exemplary practitioners of the logger's art from the time he and his sons first began to harvest the Adirondacks.

CHAPTER TWO

Emigrés from Pennyslvania

"The country is large and our operation is new,
and we are living hand to mouth, nothing fully
completed and all of us deprived of the usual customary conveniences of proper living."
—*W.L. Sykes*, 1912

"The Company has never failed; has paid its bills
promptly; has no chattell mortgages; no suits or
judgements against us."
—*W.C. Sykes*, 1931

The Emporium Forestry Company is an exceptionally fine mirror which reflects the history of Adirondack logging in 272 manuscript boxes of company papers preserved by the Adirondack Museum. These papers richly reveal the activity of a family business, an empire, which was owned and operated by the Sykes family—W. L. Sykes and his sons George W., W. Clyde and Roy O.—between 1910 and 1950. The papers are a primary record of the rigors and rewards of business in the north woods, a first-hand account of accidents and epidemics, Red scares, crime, religion, politics and prohibition, fires, wars, depressions, ethnic diversity, education, prejudice and changing times. They also provide a rare insight into the success of an individual—W. L. Sykes—who was known in his lifetime (1859-1941) as the "Hardwood King" of the Adirondacks.

In the course of its history, the Sykes' Emporium cut and processed over one billion board feet of lumber, and left a legacy, a yardstick against which can be measured the accomplishments of other companies and individuals. The Emporium Forestry Company records also give an inside picture of logging from the top, an elitist view of a hard business run by tough men which allows us to reflect on the tall tales of the woodsmen, and the romance, folklore and realities of an industry.

The woods are quiet now around the Adirondack village of Conifer, twelve miles west of Tupper Lake. The worker's houses and the larger homes on the hill are painted, comfortable looking and secure against the weather. A variety of satellite dishes here and there punctuate the open spaces between the buildings. In the summertime a knowledgeable visitor, if he looks carefully, can discern in the undergrowth a remnant of one of the large blowers from the sawmill, a railroad tie or two and the powerhouse where two Corliss steam engines drove the generators that made electricity for the mill machinery and village. As for the schoolhouse, the Conifer Inn and hemlock-board sidewalks, these are now but a memory of the years when Conifer was a thriving company village—the creation of W. L. Sykes. It was the epitome of a family-owned and family-dominated enterprise which worked the forest, turned logs into finished lumber and, in the process, made money.

William Lowther Sykes had been born in 1859 at Round Island, Pennsylvania, when the Pennsylvania and Erie Railroad was being built in Clinton County near the family home. His father was described as a skilled woodturner. At the time of his death in 1941, W. L., as he was almost always referred to, was a trustee of Syracuse University, founder and president of the Emporium Forestry Company, a director of Lumber Mutual Casualty Insurance Company and of the American Steamship Company of Buffalo. In December 1940, Dun and Bradstreet's report on the Emporium Forestry Company had listed him as principal stockholder of the firm who, although retired from active day-by-day participation in operations, still supervised the management. The report confided that he was "82, married, of English descent and for many years resided in Buffalo . . . , but now makes his home in Conifer." And, with some understatement it indicated, "He is reported to be well-to-do in his own right." His three sons were all employed by the company when W. L. died. In its report of 1942, Dun and Bradstreet noted, "This business has been in the Sykes family since 1882, and is the leader in this state." Nearly thirty years later his importance was still recognized, being referred to as "the king of the Northeastern hardwoods."

W. L. Sykes built his first sawmill at Benzinger in Elk County, Pennsylvania, in 1882, and one year later formed a partnership with

William Caflisch; they incorporated the Emporium Lumber Company in Pennsylvania in 1892. The following year, the company began operating a sawmill at Keating Summit in Potter County, which ran for twenty years (1893-1913). In 1899, Sykes and Caflisch were expanding again by building an extensive logging and sawmill business at Galeton, also in Potter County. From the time the mill started sawing in 1900, it operated around the clock, night and day until 1918. The company bought additional mills from A. G. Lyman, one at Austin, Pennsylvania and another at Portageville, in western New York, and they arranged a working alliance with a larger lumber company that was to reap great benefits. The Goodyear Lumber Company, then known as F. H. and C. W. Goodyear, had been operating sawmills in Keating Summit and Austin and owned vast acreages of timberland. But the Goodyears were hemlock manufacturers and not interested in hardwoods; their two mills in Austin were turning out such large volumes that the city became known as "Hemlock City." Along with their expanding lumber manufacturing facilities the Goodyears had an extensive network of logging railroads, much of it consolidated in 1893 to form the Buffalo and Susquehanna line.

Sykes and Caflisch realized that unlimited exploitation of Pennsylvania's forests had to end soon and, in anticipation of this, they looked both south and north for timber. Their experience had been that much of their money making had resulted from wise purchases in untried territory, i.e. fifty thousand acres in southern Vermont and some eighty thousand acres in St. Lawrence County in the Adirondacks as well as some investments in southern timber. In 1910, the Emporium Lumber Company purchased from George A. McCoy and Son of Tupper Lake an entire sawmill operation which included a sawmill building, barn, men's camp, root cellar, blacksmith's shop, cook house and an office all located at Conifer. On January 9, 1922, the contents of the buildings were inventoried. Among other things the mill contained: a horse scraper, two hundred feet of one-and-a-quarter-inch rope, two twelve-inch jack screws, an eleven-inch broad axe and a steam engine and boiler. The barn had ten horses in it, several thousand pounds of hay and straw, five sets of skidding harness, one skidding whiffletree, ten horse blankets and sundry other equipment. In the root cellar, the company's newly-acquired stores included thirty-five gallons of syrup, a quarter of beef, three-and-a-half barrels of pork, one hundred sixty pounds of codfish and a half barrel of molasses.

The blacksmith shop yielded an inventory of eighty-four separate line items, among them twenty canthooks, seven canthook handles, twenty-three canthook bands, three sets of skidding tongs, three monkey wrenches, two draw shaves, one spoke shave, one bit stock and box of bits, one two-inch auger, a boring machine, an adz, fourteen pairs of blacksmith tongs, sundry quantities of bar iron, blacksmith's coal, a wooden maul and one set of shoeing tools.

The office building contained such interesting items as large and small veterinary syringes, harness oil, a bottle of "Oil of Life," one-and-a-half bottles of colic cure, one pint of laudanum (opium), a pint of liniment and 15 dozen bottles of "Harlem Oil," together with nine spuds, an iron bed and springs, a crosscut saw, a looking glass and one alarm clock. In the office itself were the van goods (items which stocked the "company store") and which included sixty-six pounds of Payns tobacco, sixty-six pounds of cut plug tobacco, plus rubber boots, heavy shirts, cotton shirts, short rubber coats, heavy rubbers and twenty pair of yarn mitts.

The men's camp and cook's camp contained an assorted quantity of beds, blankets and mattresses (fifty double blankets in the men's camp inventory and thirty-seven in the cook's camp), plus three rocking chairs and four pack baskets; dishes and kitchen utensils for forty men, a cook stove, sausage machine, coffee grinder, mustard grinder, six bushels of peas, ten bushels of beans and two hundred pounds of prunes. Also, there were water pails, wash tubs, box stoves, sixty pounds of lard and an assortment of wall lamps and table lamps; and in a storehouse at Childwold Station (and included in the deal) were rat traps, six torches, twenty-two barrels of "Pillsbury Flour," fifteen crosscut saws, two dozen axe helves, twenty lanterns, ten canthooks, two lumber wagons, two sets of bog sleighs with whiffletrees and neck yokes, five sets of log chains (complete), six skidding chains, eight torches, eight peavies, twenty-five axes and two grindstones. Gathering supplies clearly was not a minor logistical requirement for the lumberman.[1]

In 1910, Emporium also purchased from A. A. Low of Horse Shoe, also in St. Lawrence County, "all the machinery, fixtures and appliances . . . belonging to the Bog River sawmill, planing and wood mill . . . consisting principally of an 8-ft. Clark band mill, complete," equipment and machinery made by Clark Brothers of Olean, a firm well known to Sykes. The purchase included:

"[two] large stationary boilers and fixtures complete, with settings, including masonry and bricks, and all of the pumps and piping connected in the mills, together with the dry kiln apparatus, trucks, etc., and the machinery and tools that properly belong to the woodmill, saw mill and planing mill plants, and also the large, new electric generator and belt in the power house at Bog River mill, and the wiring belonging to this generator between the generator and the mill, but not including the switch board in the power house, and also including all the electric motors and connections within the mill plants mentioned, and not including the jack mill machinery for loading logs on cars from the saw mill; it being the intention of this bill of sale to convey all the machinery, fixtures, tools and appliances not herein excepted, including belting, fire hose and saws, which may belong to the saw mill, wood mill and planing mill, whether the same be located in the buildings or elsewhere, but not including the buildings, but to include the flooring scraper and the gang flooring rip saw at the mill at Horse Shoe Station."[2]

All of the equipment and machinery was to be used in retrofitting the Conifer property and cost $15,000. The sawmill equipment was in place and operating by October 1911. The following August, Sykes was staking out the foundations for a planing mill, hoping

"... to get the buildings up within the next two months and be ready for bad weather. ... [It] now looks as if we will locate it about 200 ft. east of the saw mill up the little stream South of the boarding house, which will make it a safe distance from fire and give us cheap insurance, and will likely take the steam from the mill boilers to make power, though we may use electric motors to drive it from those we bought from Mr. Low, and in order to save steam it might be advisable to use the Corliss engine now stored at Galeton."[3]

The Sykes had come from the relative comfort of Keating Summit, Pennsylvania, and their already substantial logging and sawmill operations, to the wilds of the Adirondacks. The man known as the "Hardwood King" of the lumber business found the mountains a challenge as Emporium started operations in the north woods. In July 1912, W. L. Sykes wrote to W. M. Weston as if from the frontier that "the country is large and our operation is new, and we are living hand to mouth, nothing fully completed and all of us deprived of the usual customary conveniences of proper living."

At the time when Sykes arrived in the Adirondacks, good logging practice dictated that several weeks in the summer be devoted to exploring company lands and deciding from which tract logs for the following year would be taken. Then an owner contracted or "let the log job" to a jobber to cut all the trees in a specified area above a certain diameter. After agreements were reached, a contractor waited until the snow was sufficiently deep and then took a force of men, horses and supplies into the woods to build camps close to the cutting area.

The details of early contracts were romantically described "as the same as those used by the pioneers," meaning they were informal and sealed by a handshake. More realistically, however, contracts were precise documents specifying the amount and species of logs to be cut in what amount of time, the delivery of them to the banks of a stream or lake, and the terms for payment. In the Adirondacks, the contracts were usually let in terms of a regional unit of measure: so many thousand "standards" or "markets"—logs nineteen inches in diameter, by thirteen feet long. Elsewhere, amounts were specified by the thousand feet. When an agreement had been reached, it was written out and signed by both parties.

An actual agreement made on May 26, 1910, between Margaret Mc-Clinton, jobber, and Emporium yields considerable information as to precisely how the job was done and provides great insight into the thoroughness and control exercised by large logging operations during the first decade of the twentieth century. The contract stated:

> . . . for and in consideration of the sum or sums hereinafter named to be paid by the . . . Company . . . the . . . Jobber does hereby agree to cut into pulp-wood (or into logs, or both, if the company or its agents may direct) all the spruce, hemlock, balsam and pine trees or parts of trees which were damaged or injured by fire, or dead and down trees, which are suitable for pulp-wood or logs, and to peel and to save the merchantable Hemlock Bark or damaged trees, upon that portion of the Saxe tract of land which lies north of the Grasse River in the town of Jamestown, St. Lawrence County, New York; and do the work and receive the consideration therefore under the following terms and conditions. . . .[4]

The document was signed and witnessed by Margaret McClinton and W. L. Sykes, himself. For a woman to be the contractor or jobber was unusual. She may have been the "business manager" for a husband and/or sons who were loggers, but this is speculation. Other than the record of her contract with W. L. Sykes, no other reference to McClinton exists in the Emporium files.

Courtesy of The Adirondack Museum

William Lowther Sykes (1859-1941) was known during his lifetime as the "Hardwood King of the Adirondacks."

In 1910, the Emporium Lumber Company purchased from George A. McCoy and Son an entire sawmill operation near Tupper Lake, New York. Postcard by H. M Beach.

William Lowther Sykes and Stella Walker Sykes c. 1895.

The William Lowther Sykes family c. 1935.

The George A. McCoy Sawmill operation included a blacksmith's shop shown here in a postcard by H. M. Beach.

The powerhouse generated power for the mills and the village of Conifer. Two Corliss steam engines provided power to drive the generator.

Early living accommodations in Conifer were primitive.

Workers' houses in the village of Conifer were built for men with families.

The owners' and managers' houses were built above the mills and the workers' dwellings, a separation common to most industrial villages of the time.

The company schoolhouse, together with the company store and company housing, emphasized the paternal aspects of Conifer's management.

The Conifer Inn attracted a wide variety of guests—businessmen, sportsmen, travelers, foreign and domestic.

The jobber system was widely used in the Adirondacks and almost universally by the Emporium Forestry Company. In 1936, a bleak year in and out of the woods, J. D. Gilmour analyzed the role of jobbers and business management in general. "The old generation of lumberjacks despised pulp-wood operations. . . . They tended rather to remain with the saw-log operations, and declined in numbers through old age and other reasons. . . ." They thought cutting pulp was "farmer's work" which, in fact, it often was. According to Gilmour,

"The first pulpwood operations were small, in easy locations and in timber which had been passed over by saw-logging operations. It was, therefore, easy to find a few farmers who, at low cost, delivered pulpwood from such locations. I believe that thus the 'jobber' system must have originated. . . . Whatever the reason, the 'jobber' system became firmly established, and has cost this industry much money in direct excess costs, and much more in stagnation of development. . . . The failure has been less with the logging operators than it has been with the management of the companies, because it was entirely in their hands as to what sort of logging policy they followed, and the decision was entirely theirs as to whether they would develop and maintain permanent logging staffs who actually did the logging, or would carry skeleton staffs only, to deal with 'jobbers'. . . . The decision was taken that 'jobbers' would do the logging. . . . Jobs are let only from year to year, therefore no jobber can afford to own equipment to any great extent, if such equipment has several years' life, and represents considerable capital. He cannot be sure of profitable employment for it; the fact that he has it is a disadvantage to him, because to some extent it ties him down in bargaining. It is not feasible to move it long distances every season; besides, it will be adapted to one type of job but perhaps not so well adapted in another section. . . . It really never concerned him even though there were other methods available which would save costs to the company. He therefore lacked incentive, besides lacking both education and capital."[5]

Irrespective of the theoretical advantages or disadvantages, once the contracts were signed and the cutting areas selected, the jobber quickly erected logging camps on sites as near as possible to where the lumber was to be cut. Fox recorded that "the buildings or 'camps' are made of logs" with cracks "chinked" with moss and sticks, "to keep out the wind and the cold." The jobber, while the camp was being built, had a crew cutting a tote road to the site over which he hauled the lumber needed for the construction of buildings and "the making of the necessary partitions, doors, floors, bunks, and the log tables at which the men eat."[6]

In the early days, camps such as the one Sykes purchased from Mc-Coy in 1910, had no floors. However, by the turn of the century, most camps had flooring of boards or flattened logs. Even shingles for roofing and window sashes were carried in. The camps for larger jobs accommodated eighty to one hundred men. Generally, there was one low, large building with an attic in which there were tiers of bunks as in a barracks or dormitory. The ground floor was divided into two rooms; one section contained long tables where meals were served, the other part was partitioned off for a "lounge" where the crew sat in the evenings, smoking, reading, singing or playing cards.

Logging camps quickly grew into small villages, as was the case at Conifer. Alfred Truman, a friend of the family from Pennsylvania visiting in 1917, found the place almost bucolic. What had been "an interminable wilderness but a short time ago . . . now abounded with houses with every convenience known to modern life." In 1912 during the flurry to construct and equip Conifer, Clyde Sykes had written to W. A. Case and Son of Buffalo saying, "We are building about 15 houses and a boarding house." It was not men he wanted from Case and Son, it was "six bathroom outfits complete. We do not want the highest priced goods as these houses are being built to accommodate working men. [We] want strong, durable goods." To another firm, Conde Hardware Company in Watertown, he reminded that in July 1911, "we purchased from you two bathtubs, two lavatories and two closets complete." He asked for Conde's prices and a catalogue. He also told Conde that "at least ½ dozen of each of the above mentioned items" would probably be needed since the company wanted "to install bathrooms in a number of the houses."

There was even a schoolhouse "where-in religious services are held by a pastor whose salary is greater than that received by many who are preaching in the larger centers of population." Parroting Edward Bellamy, Truman saw Conifer as a workman's paradise. Thirty years later, John Stock, the assistant superintendent at Emporium, described the same scene.

> "Conifer was probably the last of the old-time company towns—a unique little segment of civilization located at the end of a country road. At its peak it was entirely self-sufficient, with dwellings for some fifty families, plus a hotel, boarding house, store, post office, railroad station, school, church, doctor, pool hall and soda fountain. . . . The

school boasted a principal and two years of high school. Today it would be considered a very modern upgraded setup. Then it was just an old-fashioned back-woods school, with each teacher being responsible for more than one grade. The end product was excellent."[7]

The early years of Emporium's history at Conifer were enormously busy and difficult. The Sykes, as stated earlier, had quickly upgraded the sawmill, planned the village and took on the construction of a railroad. The typescript of a press release found in the company archive from about 1911 outlines what was being done and what improvements were in the offing. Headed "Emporium Lumber Company to Erect Big Up-State Mill," it tells its readers that the company, which owned some eighty-five thousand acres in the Cranberry Lake region, was erecting a large sawmill and also was planning

> ". . . as soon as the snow is gone to construct a railroad from a point on the Mohawk and Malone division of the New York Central, either at Childwold or Piercefield, through the timber of the company to the proposed new plant and to Cranberry Lake totalling fifteen miles. . . . In addition to affording facilities for the lumbering operations of the company, the railroad will open to tourists an extensive territory in the Adirondacks heretofore inaccessible and will permit the traveler to leave New York City in the evening and partake of breakfast in Cranberry Lake."[8]

Railroads were an essential tool of the hardwood loggers (as the improved highways and trucks were later). The Sykes had had experience with railroad logging during their Pennsylvania business years particularly after they acquired the Goodyear holdings. W. L. was as much a railroader as he was a lumber baron. On July 7, 1911, the *Tupper Lake Herald* reported that, from the noise of blasting and booming of dynamite going on around Childwold, a person might easily think it was just one long continuous Fourth of July holiday. But it was not. It was the Grasse River Railroad then under construction.

It was an expensive proposition to build even two miles of track, let alone sixteen miles, the actual distance of the line. On May 23, 1911, C. W. Carlson submitted an estimate of $3,120 per mile "to build your Railroad from Childwold Station on the M and M Railroad to your mill . . . including the switches and the way that you will have to construct"—and this for just about two miles of track. Carlson did not get the job. But in June 1911, Frank Greco, who was operating in North

Carolina, presented an acceptable bid of $2,560 and was hired to build the road as far as Conifer.

The Sykes were then anxious to push it on to Cranberry Lake but Greco was still involved in North Carolina. There was considerable financial risk for the company if jobber contracts were not executed correctly and on time; cut logs had to be gotten out of the woods. W. L. Sykes wrote to Greco in 1912 that delay in building the road and tramlines was unacceptable. Sykes told him that it was important that

> ". . . you should come up here yourself so that we may see you and have a definite understanding as to the work that has been done. . . . We have over one million feet of new cut hard wood logs down at the tram-road that should be sawed before warm weather or they will spoil, so you can see the need of prompt action. This is no boy's job . . . and the conditions and circumstances confront us, over which we have no control, which compel us to take this position. The season for doing this class of work is very short up here as we experienced last year and we do not wish to be caught this year with a lot of unfinished work."[9]

Greco came to Conifer and, by June, Emporium was looking for men to finish the line, going as far afield as Williamsport, Pennsylvania to find them. Bridges had to be built as well. In August 1912, the company wrote to New Hampshire and Pennsylvania for men who could do bridge work. Finally by 1913 the railroad was completed to Cranberry Lake.

The road was never a great financial success. In its first eight years of operation (1913-1921) the economic picture varied according to the amount of lumber shipped. According to Emporium records,

> " . . . the railroad has never paid a cent in dividends and probably never will, as its life depends on the forest products along its line and it is very doubtful if they will last long enough; or if additional business will be built up in the way of summer resort trade or otherwise to keep it going. There are deposits of iron ore in this vicinity and similar iron has been commercially developed at other points in the Adirondacks on a paying basis."

There was a glimmer of optimism, but when the company took a hard look at the road's future, it seemed that "this carrier appears to be a limited life carrier on account of depletion of natural resources." By 1921, the road had a deficit of almost sixty thousand dollars.[10]

Lack of success was not for lack of trying to market and promote the

Grasse River. W. L. Sykes wanted the railroad's general manager, A. C. Stewart, to be "prepared to answer most any questions of importance that may come up in meetings or conventions or conferences with other railroads or officials that may not know the facts in connection with the Grasse River Railroad." Sykes promoted business opportunities, tourism, recreation (hunting and fishing), manufacturing, natural beauty and agricultural possibilities as potential for the Grasse River Railroad. He wanted it known that "Conifer, a thriving lumber village near the eastern end of the Railroad has saw and planing mills, dry kilns, machine shops and hotel, with a new graded school modern and up to date, general store and post office." Just four miles beyond there was the Grasse River Club and beyond that Cranberry Lake, "a village of several hundred population with two churches, graded school, large modern saw mill, several stores and post office, planing mill, and prospects of other developments. . . ." The lake, according to Sykes, was

> ". . . the largest of the Adirondack lakes and the Grasse River Railroad is the only railroad leading to Cranberry Lake, making it possible for tourists or travelers to leave Buffalo, New York, or intermediate points in the evening and take breakfast at Cranberry Lake with only one change of cars."

In addition, the railroad tapped

> ". . . several hundred thousand acres of timberlands along the Grasse River, principally owned by the Emporium Forestry Company, also the Raquette River Paper Company, the International Paper Company, the Newton Falls Paper Company and the A. Sherman Lumber Company and other land owners, and at present the Paper companies and others referred to are shipping woods products such as logs, lumber, bark, pulpwood, etc. over the Grasse River Railroad to the various markets and will continue to ship for many years to come, as much of this forest product has no other outlet except over the Grasse River Railroad."[11]

Not only was the region traversed by the railroad a hunters' and fishermen's paradise, it was also suitable for farming, grazing or dairying. It was particularly good for growing potatoes, hay and forage.

The railroad was strongly supported by private and public interests in St. Lawrence County. George Holmes, the county treasurer, was certain that the Grasse River, as a public carrier, "will be a great accommodation not only to the community of Cranberry Lake but to a multitude of city people who spend their summers, or portion of them, there.

Anything which helps any part of this country helps it all." And a wholesale grocer—Andrus-Robinson Company—attested that "a railroad thru this section is a genuine public utility, and an entire section would be absolutely inaccessible without the service which this company now affords."

On May 12, 1916, the Grasse River Railroad issued its first printed broadside of "Passenger Fares and Distances" together with rules and regulations for transporting "Baggage, Bicycles, Baby Carriages, etc., Canoes, Racing Shells, etc., Corpses, Dogs, [and] Theatrical Properties" to be effective May 15, 1916, its first day as a public carrier. The most detailed regulation was for corpses:

> "One whole first-class ticket at regular tariff fare will be required, with a minimum of $1.00, for transportation of corpse, without regard to the age of the deceased, Agents marking all coupons and stub 'Corpse.' No corpse will be received unless in charge of passenger, and accompanied by a physician's, coroner's or board of health certificate, also an undertaker's certificate that [the] body has been prepared for burial and shipment in accordance with the rules of the State Board of Health, nor will it be received even with such certificate if fluids are escaping from the case, or it has become offensive in any degree."[12]

Those who have written about the Grasse River and other Adirondack railroads have been captivated by the rolling stock and locomotives which operated on them. There was no question, as George W. Sykes wrote Henry W. Bragdon in 1959, that "steam locomotives really do seem to have personalities." There is as much nostalgia for the days of steam as for the early days of lumberjacks and log drives. The younger Sykes revealed that "the Emporium Companies and the Grasse River Railroad had a total of 23 locomotives," and over two hundred pieces of rolling stock of all types, but it was "nowhere near the truth that any of the Grasse River's engines dated back to the Wilderness Campaign or near any Civil War decade." One of the Grasse River's first engines, Road No. 33, was a Baldwin Saddle Tank 0-6-2 that had formerly been a switch engine of the Emporium Lumber Company at Keating Summit. Number 33 was sold to the St. Regis Paper Company in 1926.

The 1930s were slow years; however, the Railroad operated from Conifer to Cranberry Lake until 1948. That year the rails were removed from the right of way to the westerly end of the Conifer yard. Only the track from Conifer to Childwold remained. The following year, Heywood-Wakefield Company purchased the remaining Emporium property, including the railroad. The Grasse River had been operated by the Emporium Forestry Company from 1913 to 1948. In the end its success was the application of railroad technology as an adjunct to Emporium's hardwood logging business. It transported a billion board feet of lumber out of Cranberry Lake and Conifer, and opened what was a relatively inaccessible region to the inroads of tourists and vacationers.

On January 22, 1912, the Emporium Forestry Company was incorporated in the state of New York with $500,000 capital stock, the number of shares to be ten thousand at a par value of fifty dollars each. The principal offices were located at Conifer in the Township of Atherton in St. Lawrence county. It was no coincidence that "forestry" was incorporated in the company's name, since it connoted awareness—if not total practice—of the most avant-garde thinking in the lumber industry. Logging had progressed from an exploitative enterprise to one at least nominally influenced by the rise of forestry schools and the conservation movement of the 1880s and early twentieth century as championed by a friend of W. L. Sykes, Gifford Pinchot. In Pinchot's *Adirondack Spruce* (1898) can be found the model for "conservative logging" and forest management which was put into practice by Dr. Webb at Ne-Ha-Sa-Ne Park and at William C. Whitney's preserve above Raquette Lake. Forestry, thanks to Pinchot and his disciples, was the buzz-word of the day and Sykes knew it.

The purposes of the company were:

"To acquire, buy, sell or otherwise own, buy, sell and deal in standing timber and timberlands and to buy, cut or dry and sell timber and logs and to saw or otherwise cut the same and to buy, manufacture and sell lumber, bark, pulp wood and all other forest products or articles made therefrom. To carry on business as timber merchants, sawmill proprietors and timber growers and to buy, sell, grow, prepare for market, manipulate, import, export and deal in timber and wood of all kinds and to manufacture and deal in articles of all kind in the manufacture of which timber, wood or any other forest products are used."[13]

W. Clyde Sykes summed up the corporate entities and how they interacted in 1924 when he wrote that

". . . in 1912 the Emporium Forestry Co. was founded by the same people who owned the Emporium Lumber Co., and was officered by the same officers. This Corporation took over timber in the Adirondacks and is now operating on a tract of 120,000 acres, having mills

Company business was conducted from the office while the store or "van" provided a variety of goods for the workers.

Emporium Forestry Company staff photographed in the company office c. 1940. George W. Sykes is at the extreme right.

Lumberyard and mill at Conifer, New York. Photograph by H. M. Beach who was commissioned by W. L. Sykes.

The Company, in the course of its history, cut over a billion board feet of lumber. Aerial view of the Company c. 1940.

Emporium Forestry Company's Cranberry Lake Band Mill.

The Company's Grasse River Railroad linked Conifer to Cranberry Lake and to the New York Central at Childwold. It was indispensable in logging the Sykes' forest lands.

THE RAILS -EMPORIUM R.R. CRANBERRY LAKE N.Y.

Laying the rails for the Grasse River Railroad.

Charles Sadley, construction engineer for the Grasse River Railroad.

Locomotive No. 43 moving log train into position for loading by Barnhardt Steam Log Loader.

In addition to maintaining its milling equipment, the machine shop at Conifer serviced over 200 pieces of rolling stock of all types and twenty-three locomotives belonging to the Grasse River Railroad.

The Emporium Forestry Company issued 5,540 shares of common stock and 5,940 shares of preferred stock.

In April of 1949, Heywood Wake-field Company - furniture makers from Gardner, Massachusetts - took over the Conifer works.

Eight million board feet of lumber in the Conifer yards photographed on February 18, 1921 from the roof of the Conifer Inn.

located at Conifer, N.Y., and Cranberry Lake, N.Y. . . . In order to simplify accounting and to save inter-company records and to save inter-company transactions, the Emporium Forestry Co. will, from Jan. 1st, 1924, be the active operating Company, and all business will be done in its name."[14]

In March 1951, George W. Sykes, the oldest of the Sykes sons, estimated that in its seventy-year history both in Pennsylvania and New York state, the company had cut the following amounts at its various mills:

Mill	Time period	Approx. Cut in Board Feet[15]
Benzinger Mill	about 14 years	50,000,000
Keating Summit Mill	20 years	200,000,000
Galeton Mill	over 17 years	200,000,000
Austin Mill	about 12 years	150,000,000
Conifer Mill	about 37½ years	250,000,000
Cranberry Lake Mill	10 years	200,000,000
Total		1,050,000,000

The Emporium Forestry Company's size made it a major force in Adirondack and national logging circles. At its high point the company employed well over 280 persons of all categories and nationalities—woodsmen, mill-workers and railhands; French-Canadian, Irish, Poles, Russians, Austrians and Italians. They managed the Grasse River Railroad as both a public carrier and a necessity in getting the hardwood to the mill and the product to market. They ran a company village, owned between 140 and 150 dwelling houses and a couple of hotels. In 1931, not a good year for business, Clyde Sykes estimated the worth of the company at $3 million dollars doing an annual business (sales) in the vicinity of $700,000. "The Company has never failed; has paid its bills promptly; has no chattel mortgages; no suits or judgements against us." In 1931, not every family enterprise could make that statement.

Though in comparatively good financial condition, Emporium did have large debts and an active management style. The company's philosophy was

". . . the business of any lumber manufacturing concern owning extensive holdings of timber and timber lands . . . is, liquidation. That is liquidation of timber stumpage values, of land, and of such parts of the plant as become idle and no longer needed as the years pass, and conditions change. At times this is gradual over periods of years, and at other times, rapid, as in the case of large land sales."[16]

In the 1920s and 1930s Emporium sought fluidity through debt reduction, which meant that some portion of the massive overhead in non-productive land holdings had to be sold. Between December 1926 and June 1939, this debt reduction resulted in a liquidation of thousands of acres and an indebtedness of $1,910,686 reduced to $516,551 over the same period. Foresight and planning were the name of the game: these had paid off for Emporium since its Pennsylvania years.

In an effort to sell off a portion of its holdings so as to become less land poor and more competitive, the company prepared an enticing prospectus for a buyer or investor. It read:

> "As to accessibility, practically the whole central portion of the entire area is traversed by a logging railroad bed or 'grade' made of gravel, which can for a relatively very small expense be converted into a strictly private road for the owners or lessees of the tract and/or for a bridle path on which horseback riders can ride as much as twenty miles one way without crossing any public highway whatever. This long private road can readily be connected with the public road extending into the western part of the tract, although it is not now connected with this public road. The part of this logging railroad grade or bed nearest to Cranberry Lake and Conifer and Tupper Lake Junction is within about one hour's drive by automobile from Tupper Lake Junction, via New York State highway numbers 3 and 56 and a road used by the Hollywood and Massawepie Clubs over a long period of years (Massawepie Club being a part of this 50,000 acres). The regeneration of forest growth on this land is thrifty and has been uninterrupted by fires throughout the thirty years or more of the Emporium's ownership. The softwoods are growing into value as Pulpwood and good cuts of Pulpwood can be taken again from considerable area of this 50,000 acre tract, within a much shorter period of time than would be required for the growth of trees of sufficient size for sawlogs, considerable of it within the next ten years (1938-1948)."

The extent of this tract of the company's lands was described in a document entitled "a Contiguous Block of Adirondack Forest Land of about 50,000 acres or 75 square miles" and constituted the acreage sold to the Draper Corporation in 1945.[17]

Between 1930 and 1950, the company weathered the Great Depression, suffered through FDR and the New Deal, lost its founder and survived World War II. But in the post-war years, the handwriting was on the wall and in the ledgers. It was a new world and Emporium's owners were growing older. In the 1940s, they began the process of sell-ing the company and its mills to one of their longtime customers. Heywood-Wakefield, furniture manufacturers of Gardner, Mas-sachusetts, took over the Conifer works—mills, railroad, shops and all—from the Sykes in April, 1949. Very soon after acquiring the prop-erty,

> "... [they] rebuilt the sawmill into a unit much more efficient than the former mill, capable of sawing twelve million feet per year. New equipment was installed such as an eight-foot band mill, Prescott car-riage, Prescott band re-saw, and a jump saw trimmer. . . . The out-moded overhead lumber docks were removed and a new sorting sys-tem built. The future had a rosy glow for the inhabitants of Conifer with mill employment now up to 125 to 150. . . . But log costs had now risen excessively, and it wasn't 'like it was' during Emporium's day."[18]

In reality, the "old days" had ended with the death of W. L. Sykes in 1941. He had been the company's driving force, an inventor, innovator, and a shrewd, highly individualistic businessman. He was a typical, sometimes eccentric, product of his time, whose family, church and business were the primary concerns of his life. Had it not been for World War II, the company might well have ended sooner than it did. As things were, it took eight years for his life's work to be dissolved.

In May, 1949, George Sykes wrote to his brother Roy that, had their father lived, he would have been ninety years old. It is little wonder the boys were thinking about their father who had built the empire that they were now in the process of dissolving. In 1947 the company had begun the procedure required for a publicly-held firm to go out of busi-ness specified under New York State's Business Corporation Law gov-erning the voluntary dissolution of a stock company or corporation. Along with meeting several other technical requirements Emporium had to file a certificate with the secretary of state claiming "that the cor-poration elects to dissolve." The request for a certificate of dissolution had to be endorsed by the State Tax Commission at the time of filing, a formality presuming that there were no corporate taxes due. Once hav-ing filed, the company ceased all business operations except those neces-sary and required for the liquidation of the firm. After liquidation was completed and with no further claims outstanding against the company, it would then have to file with the county clerk a certificate of termina-tion. Ninety days thereafter, the Emporium Forestry Company would no longer exist. The entire process usually required three years from the date that the certificate was filed with the secretary of state. This process occurred at the same time Emporium was negotiating its contract and sales documents with Heywood-Wakefield. In order to get things started, the Board of Directors and stockholders approved a resolution ordering that liquidation of assets be commenced.

In Syracuse on December 19, 1947, "a Special Meeting of the Stockholders . . . voted in favor of the orderly liquidation of the corporation and conversion of its assets into cash." It was made clear, because of the accumulated dividends on the preferred stock, that all proceeds realized from turning the company's assets into cash (and after paying off debts and creditors) would go to the preferred stockholders. Nothing would go to the common stockholders "whose stock is valueless in any event." On December 26 the president of the Emporium Forestry Company wrote to its stockholders telling them that the certificate of capital reduction had been filed, and that the company was "now in a position to make the distribution of $40.00 per share to the preferred stockholders." This was payment of a liquidation dividend based upon 5,540 shares of common (par value $1.00) and 5,940 of preferred stock (par value $100 each). As of June 30, 1947, an audit report prepared by Marshall Granger and Company of New York had shown the firm's assets to be $693,083.61. It is significant that between 1924 and 1945 the amount of timberland held by Emporium had dropped to 74,664 acres and that this reduction had been a conscious effort to reduce its bonded indebtedness. In light of the firm's later history, the early decision to reduce nonproductive landholdings was farsighted and, given the condition of the economy and the industry, good management as well.

The liquidation process continued. The assets of the firm were carefully converted into cash and distributed among the holders of preferred stock. It was a slow and tedious process and not always easy or pleasant, particularly when assets of the firm for such a long period of time (1892 to 1950) had been so inextricably bound up in the affairs of the families and heirs of the original founders and partners—W. L. Sykes and William Caflisch. Business affairs were moving to a close when Mrs. Helen Heltman and her husband Professor H. J. Heltman (heirs of the estate of William Caflisch) decided to file an objection involving a sum of $42,000 which they felt was due them for the return of some 420 shares of stock in 1941. In the days of W. L. and Caflisch, such a disagreement would have been hard fought but in the end settled "within the family, not on the street." The Heltmans, apparently not getting what they felt was a fair and equitable settlement, "retained Larry Sovik to appear for them," an event which caused Ben Shove, Emporium's attorney, to tell Clyde Sykes that this was too bad, since "Sovik is a savage fighter for his client and is quite ruthless." On March 3, 1949, Shove lamented: "I am afraid that we are in for quite a legal battle." Finally, between March and July 12, 1949, the issue was settled at "a special meeting of the stockholders . . . held in "Parlor G, Onondaga Hotel, Syracuse, New York" at one-thirty in the afternoon.

It must have been a painful meeting for Clyde Sykes and his brothers as he asked for a stock vote on the following resolution:

> Resolved, that this corporation, Emporium Forestry Company, forthwith dissolve, and be it further RESOLVED, that the President or Vice President and the Secretary or Assistant Secretary are hereby authorized and directed to execute and file a certificate of Dissolution pursuant to Article 10 of the Stock Corporation Law.

E. J. Jones, one of the two original trustees still surviving and the company's general counsel, seconded the motion. No stockholders voted against the motion, and it was adopted. Present at this meeting were George W. Sykes, W. Clyde Sykes, Roy O. Sykes, Chester Sykes (W. L.'s cousin Frank's son), E. J. Jones, A. L. Owen (the second remaining original trustee), and Helen and Prof. H. J. Heltman; Charles E. Bowers, attorney for the corporation; Benjamin E. Shove, counsel for the corporation; and J. C. Bronner, attorney for Herkimer County. The group was told that $30,000 in assets remained to be liquidated. Three months later, George Sykes appeared in the office of Charles Bowers at Canton and gave a formal deposition in which he assigned the Emporium Forestry Company's remaining assets ($30,000) for one dollar to the Emporium Lumber Company of Galeton, Pennsylvania, the parent firm of the Forestry Company. One year after the Syracuse meeting on July 29, 1950, Clyde Sykes executed the application for Consent to Dissolution, and the Emporium empire was over.

During their thirty-nine years in the Adirondacks, the emigrés from the forests of Potter County, Pennsylvania had built an emporium of work, life and culture. Their attorney, E. J. Jones, had written in 1912 that "the Emporium . . . can see a dollar in a hardwood tree quicker than any other person or corporation in the business today." The long history of the family in Pennsylvania and the Adirondacks proved his point. The business of logging was to make money. The Sykes did this. They made friends, too, as they worked the woods, logged the Adirondacks and became part of the fabric of the mountains and their diverse society.

CHAPTER THREE

Diversity
Among the Pines

"I have 50 good Experience woodsmen. Nationalities are: Russians, Polls, Finns, Swedes, Natives
and others as you preferrer."
  —*United Labor Agency to Clyde Sykes*, May 1919

"We always have plenty of food but it isn't
always fresh and many a time absolutely unfit to
eat; the meat . . . in the last few days has been
absolutely rotten."
  —*Employees to Clyde Sykes*, March 1921

Camps, tools and techniques were constantly changing and improving at Conifer, but what of the men and women who moved through
the history of this epoch, not only at Emporium but elsewhere? The
logging really began when everything was in place and the jobber and
his men arrived at the company's several camps for the season, "groups
of hardy looking men, most of whom, having spent their previous earn-
ings in some metropolis of the wilderness," had no choice but to spend
another hard season in the camps.

Professor A. B. Recknagel of Cornell wrote in his *Forests of New
York* (1923), with the industry in decline, that "lumbermen have always
been strong men, physically and in character." He went on to say that
they have a sturdiness which "inheres in the hazardous enterprise of
getting out logs and making them into lumber." There was "no 'soft job'
in any part" of logging as a way of life. "The lumber-jack—the worker
in the woods—has always been a romantic figure in the popular eye."
But to Recknagel, who knew the woods worker,

"... the actual facts of his life are not romantic. ... He does his work as a matter of course, whether it be felling the trees, drawing the logs to the 'landing,' or driving them down the turbulent streams of early spring. The lumber-jack of Northern New York is a man of hardihood and of self-reliance. He lives under crude conditions which to most city dwellers would be actual hardships. He is often endangering his life by the exigencies of his work. The rivers of the Adirondacks could tell many an heroic tale—not all of the distant past."[1]

Lumbermen came up the tote road each season chewing tobacco and swapping yarns, often having walked great distances through the snow to get into camp. For many this last bit of travel was the end of a vastly different journey. In 1890, about one-third of the work force in New York's north woods was foreign-born. In 1915, a local person observed that "woodsmen are of many nationalities: Irish, English, American, Spanish, Norwegian, French Canadian, American Indian, Lithuanian, Polish, Russian, Italian, German, and Rumanian." It was a veritable league of nationalities, a Babel among the pines. The Raquette River Paper Company had two large pulpwood camps near the Oval Wood Dish Corporation camps behind Kildare near Tupper Lake. One of these was run by James Sullivan of South Colton. The crews in both of these camps were largely made up of rugged Russians who had left Russia in the period of the Bolshevik Revolution and had come to the Adirondacks. They knew very little English so communication in the religious services and in other contacts became somewhat difficult. These men remained in the Adirondack camps, learned the language and became excellent woodsmen. One logging operator later remarked, "If you want a job well done, get a Russian."

In the years immediately preceding World War I, logging camps in the Adirondacks numbered over one hundred and fifty. During the Great Depression, that number fell to about twenty with a proportionately large number of men out of work. By 1940, on the eve of World War II, the industry had once again picked up. Sixty camps now operated in the mountains and employed some three thousand persons. The ethnic composition of the lumberjack community had changed very little, and as the wartime logging programs expanded, more and more men came from northern New England, Pennsylvania and West Virginia.

By 1952, most of the foreign-born workers in Hamilton County were of Canadian descent; by 1979, the work force was still polyglot. In a "Profile of a New York Logger," the compilers revealed:

> "Timber harvesters are of all nationalities and backgrounds. They may
> be of French Canadian, Indian, Black, Asian, or of other national ori-
> gin. Probably you thought of loggers as men; but some loggers are
> women. Active loggers range in age from their teens to their 70s and
> may be even older."[2]

Sixty years earlier, W. Clyde Sykes of the Emporium Forestry Company thought "that Poles, Austrians and Swedes" made the best mill
men, particularly those men who came directly from New York City.
"It may be," he said in writing to his metropolitan office, "that you can
get in touch with some of the immigration authorities and let them
know that a few men can be used at this point." He did not want "too
big a bunch of men, particularly at once;" however, he thought maybe
"25 or 30 men . . . around the sawmills and to complete our woods tram
road work" would be just about the right number. Several months prior
to writing this, Sykes had received the following information from the
United Labor Agency at 231-33 Bowery in New York City where
"sawmill, pulp mill and woodsmen [are] our specialty," and "prompt
attention our motto." They informed him in the spring of 1919 that
they had "50 good Experience [sic] woodsmen. Nationalities are: Russians, Polls [sic], Finns, Swedes, natives and others as you prefer. If you
desire to have them, kindly answer." Charles Sisson of the Sherman
Lumber Company wrote from Potsdam to Sykes that "there are thousands of idle men looking for employment." We can "fill our camps
with good foreign labor" at between $35.00 and $50.00 per month and
thus avoid the high cost of domestic workers."

The Sykes were paying their men, depending upon skills and the
nature of the work, from $1.50 per day with board to around $3.00, and
this for a minimum of ten and often a twelve-hour day. A log scaler
made 27¢ per half an hour "on an eleven hour basis," and his board was
estimated "in the neighborhood of $4.50 a week." The purchasing
power of these wages can be compared to the cost of every-day items
such as food. In 1912 potatoes were 38¢ per bushel, onions $1.00,
turnips $1.60; and cabbages 8¢ each. Seven years later, in 1919, two pack-
ages of tapioca cost 28¢; three pounds of bacon $1.30; a can of lima beans
20¢; a can of beets 17¢; and one case of salmon $8.64.[3]

There were efforts on the part of large operators to set standard
wages in the Adirondacks. When times were uncertain, as they were

throughout the country in 1919, owners in the North Country felt they had "to establish a wage . . . considerably less than last year owing to the uncertain conditions." They reminded themselves that "in the woods we have to board men so they can have no cry about the high cost of living." In September 1920, Clyde Sykes wrote to F. M. Churchill of Rochester to thank him for sending men to Conifer. Then he pointed out that "there is some misunderstanding, however, as the rate of pay as these fellows all expect is $5.00 per day or 50¢ per hour." Sykes stated that "our scale of wages is 45¢ and up and in some cases where men are not exceptionally good we are paying a little under 45¢," and requested that Churchill "please correct this with the Labor Bureau in Rochester."

While wages fluctuated with the times, and an ethnic mix was common, there was still an uneasy feeling about "foreigners." Nelson Samson found that as late as 1952 "men from some central and Southern European countries are easily influenced by . . . agitators and are subject to all of those rallying calls of labor organizers." He reflected further that "they . . . often keep the entire camp in a turmoil." Earlier, in 1919, at the height of U.S. Attorney General A. Mitchell Palmer's deportation of radical groups, the Emporium Forestry Company received a letter warning that

> " . . . certain labor cliques known as Bolshevik, Reds and I.W.W. [Industrial Workers of the World] are seriously agitating and creating dissatisfaction among the Foreign classes of labor . . . but it is both unfair and unjust to pay the same wages to a scheming agitator, who through his insidious propaganda restricts production and sows the seeds of discontent among loyal workers."[4]

However, the men going up the tote road to Conifer or elsewhere for winter's work, or those of a later vintage who arrived by truck and went home in the evenings, were not much influenced by agitators and organizers. Unlike many other parts of the country, the working class did not frighten the middle class since Adirondack logging communities tended to be but one group or class—those who worked. While the I.W.W. (Industrial Workers of the World) and other unions found a fertile field in logging operations of the far west during the teens and twenties, the small and highly individualistic loggers or jobbers in the Adirondacks were little influenced by the labor movement. Most attempts to unionize Adirondack woods workers failed because the peak of Adirondack logging pre-dated the rise of unskilled unionism; group activity was an anathema, and from the first there was a basic sense of security which existed among men willing to work in the woods. In 1979, *The Northern Logger and Timber Processor*, albeit a trade publication, noted that even at this late date "nine out of ten loggers were against forming a labor union."

If the work force was diverse, many other aspects of the logger's life were monotonously the same. Throughout the hundred years from 1850 to 1950 that saw the rise and fall of Adirondack logging, such constants as rough bunks, bugs and lots of pork were an unvarying Adirondack standard all their own.

Ferris Meigs, president of the Santa Clara Lumber Company, was a major force in Adirondack logging. He recalled camps of the 1880s and how they were put together. When the plans for the season were set

". . . a small crew, usually in July or August, would be sent into the territory to be logged, under the Camp Foreman, to build the 'set' of camps, and cut out and construct the 'tote' road. The material for both was at hand, except for a few boards and tar-paper to be used for the roofs. No hardware was used; the hinges of doors, and the like, being made of wood on the ground. A few lights of glass to be set into the openings in the logs, cut for the purpose, were used in place of windows. The glass was left out until winter set in. The camps were made, whenever possible, of hardwood logs as these were considered less valuable than softwood logs. These logs were notched at the ends, piled one on top of another, the corners fitted together, making a solid ponderous building. The roof was made of heavy log rafters to carry the load of snow, and covered by boards and roofing paper."

Sleeping arrangements in the camps were certainly not first class. Meigs recalled that

" . . . the bunks were made of rough boards on which a canvas tick filled with straw was spread, and also a heavy, very heavy, blanket or two, usually half cotton and some 'shoddy.' No pillows or sheets—not then. In the sleeping camp, the bunks were always double-deckers to accommodate fifty to sixty men. A huge cast iron box stove furnished the heat, and as the men were in the freshest of air all day long, they slept with little or no ventilation in the camp at night. The effect can be better imagined than described. On cold frosty mornings when the door of the camp was opened, and the clear dry air rushed in, the foul air, collected during the night, would rush out, forming a veritable cloud at the doorway."

In the period between World Wars I and II, the camps were not materially different in either architecture, construction or protocol than those described in the 1880s.

In the mess camp, cooking was fairly standardized as was the diet, the accoutrements of eating and the protocol observed at table. Meigs describes all three: first in importance was

> " . . . a rule of the mess camp, which was strictly adhered to, . . . that no conversation should be indulged in when the crew was eating. A queer sight, that. Sixty men, hungry and well behaved, but not a sound, except the rattle of iron two-tined forks, and iron spoons on tin dishes and cups. The food was good and abundant, clean and nourishing; varied with the season, but always well prepared and plenty for all. The camp pig was well fed, too."[5]

The recollection of Romeo L. Arsenault of Tupper Lake, who died in 1986 at the age of 83, reinforced those of others. In the 1930s, when Arsenault worked for Finch-Pruyn and Company in and around Newcomb,

> " . . . the men lived in large log buildings, one housing the cooking and eating facilities, another the sleeping quarters (earlier Adirondack lumber camps were usually two-story buildings with cooking and eating facilities downstairs and sleeping quarters upstairs). The men washed up and cleaned their clothes in a shed-like area between the two buildings which contained a small wood stove with a large pot on it to heat the water, sinks with cold running water, wash tubs, and wash boards. Romeo called this room the 'dingle' which was a carry-over from early camps. The 'dingle' was originally a storage room between the cooking and eating area."[6]

Until the use of the insecticide DDT became widespread during and after World War II (it was not used in the Adirondacks until 1946), bedbugs and lice were part of the written and oral history of the mountain logging camps. Folklorist Robert Bethke confirms in no uncertain terms that the creepy, crawly critters evoked passionate and often times colorful responses and descriptions. He wrote

> "One hazard was the continual nuisance of bedbugs and human body lice. Men alternately cursed them and made sport of their presence. There was need to relieve the very real anxieties occasioned by the pests. Indeed, loggers were inclined to evaluate operations and individ-

ual camps largely in terms of the annoyance."

Bethke asked lumberjack Eddie Ashlaw about lousy sleeping conditions and he got a vivid response:

> "We were cuttin' wood for the Newton Brothers at Raquette Lake,
> . . . the goddamn bedbugs were so thick on the bunks they were hung
> all on haywires, each of the four corners of the bed. And still they'd
> run the ceiling and jump on you, them friggin' body lice as big as that.
> . . . Why, shit, there's no need trying to get rid of them—too many!"

Bethke also records Hamilton Ferry's bout with the bugs in the 1920s around Childwold. Ferry remembered that it had been a rough winter, but the lice were more memorable than the cold. They were "the biggest lice I ever seen in my life. Honest to Jesus, they were almost as big as my little fingernail. Body lice. I was plastered with the goddamn lice."[7]

Camp food vied for equal time with the lice in logging lore. In 1872, a brief description "of the fare" made few mouths water.

> "Fat pork, the fattest of the fat is the lumberer's luxury, which . . .
> constitutes the staple of their consumption. The drippings from a slice
> of pork, roasted before the fire, are allowed to fall on the hard tack,
> which is then dignified by the name of buttered toast; sometimes the
> pork is eaten raw, dipped in molasses (a mixture which has no equal
> except ray oysters and brown sugar). On these alone the hungry
> woodsman makes many a delicious meal, which is proof of the good
> appetite and digestion of the hardy loggers. But as the lumberers carry
> their rifles with them, to their usual supplies are occasionally added
> partridge, a bear, or a deer."[8]

William McLoughlin, in describing the logging operations of Frank A. Cutting around Lake Ozonia between 1882 and 1922, recalled a more wholesome variety of camp food. According to McLoughlin, "two cows were located at each camp" to assure fresh milk daily. He added that

> " . . . Many pigs supplied fresh pork as they were butchered along
> with sheep and lambs from Center Camp. Beef came from farmers and
> western beef from Armour and Company. The cooks were very busy
> people during the winter with so many hungry men to feed. There
> were two huge cooking stoves (wood-burning) kept in constant use.
> Bread was baked every day along with baked beans, fried salt pork
> with thick cream gravy. Carrots, beets and turnips were the fresh veg-
> etables provided, having been kept in the frost-free root cellar after

Photograph by the Reverend Aaron Maddox who frequently noted the ethnic and religious diversity of the lumberccamps.

"Woodsman No. 2" *c. 1936 by Amy Jones.*

The sanitary conditions in the lumbercamps left much to be desired. Photograph by the Reverend Aaron Maddox.

Lumbercamp construction was purely functional, constructed of materials readily at hand. Photograph by the Reverend Aaron Maddox.

Food in the lumbercamps was often distinguished by its quantity rather than its quality.

The rule of silence was observed in lumbercamp messhalls such as this one at Gould Lumber Company.

Tableware and eating utensils were simple and sturdy. Photograph by the Reverend Aaron Maddox.

Fresh pork was a familiar staple of the logger's diet. Photograph by the Reverend Aaron Maddox.

It was Aaron Maddox' contention that the presence of women as cooks brought a degree of civility to the camps. Photograph by the Reverend Aaron Maddox.

"A Good Story" by Seneca Ray Stoddard. After a hard day's work the bunkhouse was often a place for tall tales and good stories.

Music helped lighten the otherwise dreary surroundings of the bunkhouse. Photograph by the Reverend Aaron Maddox.

Adventure stories in popular weekly magazines dramatized the life and work of loggers. Fame and Fortune Weekly, *September 15, 1922.*

being grown at the camp during the summers. The filling for pies came in twenty-five pound pails. The men called it "Tamarack pie" as the pails were made of this forest product. The basic menu for all week was meat, potatoes, baked beans, pie, and frequently pancakes and doughnuts. During the winter boxes of frozen fish were shipped in from Boston and provided variety to the ususal fare."[9]

In March 1921, on the other hand, employees of the nearby Emporium Forestry Company complained that "we always have plenty of food but it isn't always fresh and many a time absolutely unfit to eat." Still another point of view was expressed by Harry Jackson when he related in 1960 that "the meals around camp or at the cook wagon were tremendous." He felt that "the food was plain but nutritious and plenteous. The basic foods were coffee, baked beans, and bread. If the cook wagon could get to a good location, additional foods were prepared. At one meal it is reported a crew of forty loggers ate a bushel of boiled eggs (at least 400), three hams, and uncounted loaves of bread."

Presumably, as the camps became less primitive, the food improved. Women began being employed as lumber camp cooks in the 1890s, which resulted in designated areas for men. William Fox stated that the crews were not allowed in the kitchen or eating room except at mealtimes and "a violation of this rule . . . [was] apt to evoke the displeasure of the cooks, and a dipperful of hot water as a penalty for 'snoopin' around the kitchen and talking to the women folks." Still, women were the exception and, in Adirondack camps, cooks were generally French Canadian men with a male assistant or helper frequently referred to as the "cookee."

In 1915, the Rev. Aaron Maddox, a "sky pilot" missionary making his circuit of the Adirondack logging camps, commented on the moral tone women camp cooks brought to the nearly all-male environment.

"In some camps women do the cooking, and here and there families are found. The foremen will sometimes bring in their wives and children. The tone of the camps is better for the presence of women, and some of these women stay in the woods for weeks at a time. To do the cooking for twenty to fifty men, especially during the log hauling, when breakfast is served at four o'clock in the morning and the last teamster is often not in until seven at night, is no easy job. Yet many of these women are most efficient, and it is the testimony of all the missionaries that their cooking is never excelled by the men."

However, the women served poor meals too and, when they did, they heard about it.[10]

Food consumption was prodigious regardless of who cooked it, for "the men . . . had to cram in enough calories to last until they came back to camp at night." There was the constant reminder that to a

> "city worker, food consumption at a woods camp is unbelievable. . . . one day's supply of flour is estimated at 250 pounds. 150 pounds of potatoes are necessary each day and if eggs are served at a meal, the cook needs 32 dozen to go around. Should chicken be on the menu, it would take 125 pounds to feed the crew for one single meal. Thirty pies are necessary for one meal while 20 dozen doughnuts will go around only once."[11]

Men worked where the food was good and the word quickly got out when cooks were incompetent. Whether "bad" equated more to quantity than quality has always been a matter of opinion. If the food was good, men accepted many of the other hardships of life in the woods.

The buildings in the logging camp, in addition to the cookhouse, usually included a one-story log barn for the horses, running gear and feed; a blacksmith's shop of log construction with a forge where shoes were made for the horses, chains were mended and tools and sleds repaired; and, in the larger camps, an office where the boss, log scaler and time keeper stayed. The offices also contained a store or van where the men bought mittens, socks, shoes and tobacco.

In the company store, according to Ferris Meigs, the men found enough essentials to supply only their basic needs. In most cases, men would "run a tab" until the next pay day. Vans carried

> " . . . an assortment of goods, patent medicines, and clothing . . . 'Pain Killer,' the genuine Perry Davis brand, was in large evidence, and plug and smoking tobacco, socks, shirts, and pants—all, but the medicine and tobacco, were made of the heaviest wool. Some of this wool, an evil burning element, seemed to find its way into the tobacco."[12]

O. F. Edwards of the Emporium Forestry Company, in 1920, wrote a prospective employee coming to work in the Adirondacks that he "should have plenty of good warm woolen clothes and shoes." He said it was difficult to tell anyone "as to just the outfit they should have for this climate." Forty years later, the requirements had become a bit more precise. The typical modern logger wears

> " . . . a torn sweat shirt which has been patched many times, a pair of

coveralls with cuffs torn off at the top of his calked boots (this pre-vents his cuffs from getting caught by brush when he needs to move fast; if his pants catch in the rigging, they will tear), and a dented tin hat which lends some protection from minor injury from sticks, rig-ging and rocks."[13]

The turn of the century scene must have been far more colorful. It was a memorable sight in Tupper Lake when a buckboard full of loggers having an uproariously good time rounded the corner. The old timers had their own dress code:

" . . . stagged pants above or just below the boot tops. Their boots were Croghan or Chippewa, with or without cauks [sic]. The pants were dirty and baggy, held up by yellow suspenders. . . . Most of them wore long underwear or union suits, one hundred percent wool in winter and cotton in the summer."[14]

Fashion plates they were not, although the variation of the "uniform" made them a colorful lot in "their heavy woolen shirts, crossed by the broad suspenders, the red of their sashes or leather shine of their belts, their kersey trousers 'stagged off' to leave a gap between the knee and the heavily spiked 'corked boots.' "

His clothes, like his food, made the lumberjack as distinctive as the cowboy on the range. His earliest patterns of eating, dressing and speak-ing remain among the strongest folk elements of an occupational group whose old ways ended with the phasing out of the logging camps and introduction of mechanized logging in the Adirondacks in the 1950s.

The men who arrived in camp in the early days, before trucks and improved roads made coming and going easier, were a mixed bunch. Not a few were

Old and ugly, dirty and tough,
Talking vulgar, ornery and gruff.

They were a hardy group and when they worked, they worked like dogs;

Their arches are broken, their fingers bent,
For years of hard work they don't have a cent.

And, as has been so often written about the Adirondack logger, when they finished working,

They spend their wages for wine and women and song,
And destiny will lead them to where they belong.[15]

They let their hair and beards grow, worked from sun-up until nightfall and "generally kept at it a couple of months, then lit out for town, stayed until they were broke, and came back to camp to make another stake." The logger as a person has remained a rather consistent composite. Until very recent times almost everyone who has described him has covered the same ground.

> "The most outstanding feature is that he is a gambler. The owner gambles everything he owns each time he starts a new show and he trusts in his own ability, ambition and drive to make it succeed. The men gamble their lives and health every day. They all have an inborn love of danger and excitement; they are highly competitive; they are braggards; and often they are vulgar."

After the industry became more mechanized, loggers often retained their earlier traits.

> "They like the challenge of big machines and big logs. They lack formal education, but this in itself can be deceiving for they are in no way an unintelligent group of men. They are highly ingenious and inventive. Although they face death every day, they seem to have no fear of it. We often find that they have sharp but often gruesome sense[s] of humor."[16]

The Rev. Frank Reed, editor of *The Lumber Camp News* and a missionary sky pilot, said the "old-time lumberjack was a strong, rugged, highly-skilled man who was dedicated to work. The bunkhouse was home. It was here he slept, visited on winter evenings, sometimes played a game of cards . . . , read a magazine . . . and wrote letters on occasion." It was not always serene as the Rev. Aaron Maddox related. The name of Jesus Christ was evoked in many a sermon around the lumber camps, but it was a name "heard all too frequently used by the men in cursing and profanity." Some things have changed very little in the mountains.

Perhaps the image of an individual logger can best be conveyed through the life of a man such as John D'Avignon. He died at Tupper Lake in October, 1950 at the age of seventy-five. John was described as "one of the last of the old time lumbermen and a prominent figure in the logging industry in the Tupper sector for nearly 60 years." He can stand as a symbol for many whose careers were neither quite so illustrious as his nor so long but who nevertheless labored a lifetime in the woods. D'Avignon was

. . . born at Clayburg, N.Y., January 9, 1874, the son of John and Sarah

D'Avignon, he began working on logging jobs in this area as a boy of 16, and during nearly 60 years of Adirondack operations, he is said to have cut more pulpwood than any other single jobber or contractor in the history of the north woods. As a young man, he lumbered for Turner in the Derrick area; subsequently he logged for A. A. Low at Horseshoe, for the Nehasane Forestry Co. at Nehasane; for the International Paper Co. at Newcomb and Ticonderoga; for Johnston at Meacham Lake, and for Johnston and Strife at Brandreth Lake. Mr. D'Avignon handled lumbering jobs for the Oval Wood Dish Corporation throughout this sector; at Whitney Park, for Sisson and White; at Litchfield Park for McCarthy Brothers, and numerous others. An able woodsman, he is remembered by lumbermen in this area for his readiness to tackle any logging job, regardless of how rugged the country involved, and for his ability to make a comeback after setbacks which would have put a less capable operator out of business for keeps.[17]

D'Avignon personified what is so often referred to in logging reminiscences as the character of the Adirondack logger. Labor turnover in the woods was historically a problem with groups of men constantly coming and going. It tended to make the lumberjack a migrant worker of sorts. The work seldom allowed for either normal family or community life or even modest participation in local politics. If a person wanted employment, he had to be ready to move from a cutover area to an uncut one. As in all seasonal industries, the work force was transient. Because of this, many workers were left without close ties to either their employers or nearby communities.

Lack of strong community ties was exacerbated by hiring practices. In many cases, men were hired by company clerks or foremen who paid little or no attention to a person's past record. They "took someone on" because they needed a body. There was also a practice in North County villages which harkened back to the press-gang tactics once employed in seaport towns. Nelson Samson outlined this in 1952 when he cited the role of personnel placement officer played by taxicab drivers.

> "Many contractors have working agreements with taxicab drivers in towns which are frequented by lumberjacks who are drunk or who have spent all of their money and drive them, often long distances, to logging camps. The contractor pays the cab fare and has himself a new man when he sobers up enough to go to work. In almost every camp visited, someone was found who had started work in his present job in just that manner."

Shanghaiing lumberjacks was a nasty practice. Unfortunately, Samson does not tell us what the cab driver got per man beyond the cab fare.[18]

By the 1970s, the man with the powersaw was considered by some the "most important person" in the logging industry. George Fowler, associate editor of *The Northern Logger and Timber Processor*, suggested in 1973 that the man with the chainsaw was industry's most vital operative.

> "Once his proficiency with the chainsaw is established, we must adequately reward him for the skill and services he provides. These rewards would take form in adequate pay (including a nearly complete repudiation of the piece work mode of pay substituting the hourly method), more fringe benefits, a guaranteed yearly employment with paid vacations, and other options which need to be explored at a later date. The forest industry must take an active interest in the role of the wood cutter. He must be recognized as the person who operates the chainsaw and who must make important decisions in the field which can affect the profitability of the operation. His image has been dulled in the past but he now must be recognized as one of your most important people."[19]

In the last half of the twentieth century, with chainsaw in hand, the logger and his work continued. He emerged not as a Paul Bunyan, macho character, but rather as the most essential element in a heavy industry who in the Adirondacks did not keep pace with the rapid technical and social innovations which had occurred in other major American industrial settings or with logging operations in other parts of the United States. The logging industry, as did the tanning, retained an image of technological conservatism.

The mention of the term "lumberjack" traditionally conjures the picture of a crude, rough, uncouth person who worked hard, got paid little above the poverty level and cut down trees in remote mountainous areas. He was, thanks to many Victorian descriptions, seen as ignorant, lazy, uninfluenced by education and most often a drinker and fighter of legendary capacity. Adventure stories were intended to quicken the pulse of urban readers. Taken with a grain of salt, accounts of logging in the popular literature were partially accurate; mostly, however, they obscured the reality of the logger's life. Scan the pages of *Harper's Weekly Magazine*, the *Atlantic Monthly*, *Scribner's*, *Blackwood's*, *Lippencott's* and a score of others, and you'll find them full of articles on Adirondack logging, new techniques, the life of the wood cutter, and the high drama of river drives. Over five hundred articles appeared in the periodical literature between 1884 and 1932 dealing with Adirondack and northeast logging and woods-related topics such as great fires, conservation, scientific forestry, and time-study analyses of the woods worker like those by F. W. Taylor. This is at once both an index to the national importance of the subject matter and a clue, in an ever-expanding urban environment, to the hold that the natural grandeur of the mountains, trees and the wilderness had on the popular mind in America. To the Victorian American, the lumberjack, in the depth of the wilderness, was like Captain Ahab in his quest on the boundless ocean, a man placed in mortal combat against the unrelenting forces of nature.

Stewart Edward White's *Blazed Trail Stories* (1904) and *The Riverman* (1908); the two-volume memoir of Ferris J. Meigs, long-time president of the Santa Clara Lumber Company (1888-1938); and the rather pessimistic outlook of L. E. Chittenden's *Personal Reminiscences* (1893) preserve a marvelous mixture of excitement, nostalgia and fact about the lumberjack. As the twentieth century wore on, *The Lumber Camp News* (1939-1952) and its successors *The Northeastern Logger* (1952-1963) and *The Northern Logger* (1963-) followed the course of the industry and its people, and defined in their own way, who the lumberjack was in articles and editorials that chronicled the practices and issues of the day.

Dramatic change has occurred in the Adirondack logging industry since 1850. The dirt roads are mostly gone, lumberjacks do not live in remote camps, and no longer are woods workers isolated or sheltered from the blight of urban life. Machines—the truck, the chainsaw, the tractor and the loader—have eased the work-day routine. Radio, television, telephones, shopping centers and super-highways have made the lumberjack an industrial worker. He has exchanged his stocking cap for a hard hat. But even with the advent of mechanized logging, it is unlikely that he will ever outlive his traditional image as a folk-character able to clear forests with a single blow of his axe, outdrink an army of "normal" folk, out-swear a mule-skinner and out-fight a pack of bears. Today, you will have to look very hard to find this person. It may well be that he existed only as a caricatured composite—the heir of John Henry the steel-drivin' man, Davy Crockett the consummate woodsman and Mike Fink the American frontier hero.

CHAPTER FOUR

The Realities of Utopia

"I hear remarks to the effect that there is more liquor
now than before the days of prohibition."
—*W. L. Sykes*, Conifer, 1920

"There are a few Catect families up here that just
abuse me. I can't go on the porch with out they call
us prodeson sun bitches. . . ."
—*Village resident*, Conifer, 1920

Logging transformed the wilderness by bringing the hustle and bus-
tle of human energy and drama into the woods. The wilderness became
a stage where strong men flourished and where the realities of harsh
terrain and bitter cold were often romanticized by those who, in their
later years, viewed monumental hardship in the rosy glow of self-
satisfaction, nostalgia and humor. Fighting, drinking, differing religious
beliefs and family feuds frequently obscured what seemed to some out-
siders a utopia.

One by one, each in its own time, the lumber towns of the Adirondacks were transformed from primitive, isolated sawmilling operations
to thriving, accessible industrial crossroads. Such was the transforma-
tion, on a smaller scale, at Conifer brought on by Emporium. In 1917,
Alfred Truman, a successful lumberman from Brookville, Pennsylvania
and a friend of the Sykes family since the 1880s, visited Conifer.

"I left home during a spell of exceedingly warm weather and
[noticed] a continuous lowering of temperature until the Adirondack

country was reached. . . . Before sunrise the train, on its way to Montreal, Canada, stopped at Childwold Station, a station standing solemnly and alone by the track which penetrates a long distance through a straight wall on either side of tall, slender evergreen trees, consisting of Cedar, Spruce and the beautifully symmetrical Balsam Fir."

Truman left the train at Childwold and was "soon conveyed to the now busy center of Conifer over a railroad built and owned by the Emporium Lumber Company, a Company known here in the Adirondacks as the Emporium Forestry Company, whose road continues on through fifteen miles of forest and open plains to Cranberry Lake. . . ."[1]

Truman had been at Conifer before, and the village's progress impressed him.

> "When I wrote from the Adirondacks only two years ago, Conifer was then in its infancy and now it is a center of unusual activity. In its very midst is the sawmill—below which is piled millions of feet of lumber—and just on the fringe of the still-natural forest stands the planing mill with its electrically driven machinery. On another side are great storage buildings and near to them extensive machine shops, where men are engaged repairing locomotives and all manner of construction work peculiar to our modern methods of lumbering where the affairs of a great business are involved. Surrounding the lines of business action, and in the shade of the larger forest trees, where green grass under cultivation now grows, there are the prettily built and painted homes of those who are there to labor and also for those who direct the operations. Many of these homes, although standing in what was part of an interminable wilderness but a short time ago, have now every convenience known to modern life, and in their very midst stands the school house. . . ."[2]

Truman was impressed that Conifer's isolation was a thing of the past. The village had turned into a veritable cultural center and

> " . . . in glancing over the hotel register I see where the addresses of guests read: Paris, France; New York; Panama; Los Angeles; Washington; Detroit; Mobile, Ala.; Wilmington, Del.; Baltimore, Md.; Montreal, Canada; Boston, Mass.; and so far away as Houston, Texas. And now that access to the great lake is made easier and with greater comfort, so will its popularity grow and its thousands of visitors yearly increase."[3]

The roster of visitors was impressive, and through Truman's rose-colored glasses, the entire workplace seemed a utopia. He was especially taken with the newest installation, a sawmill built that year at Cranberry Lake.

> "The view from the mill is most romantic, looking over the beautiful expanse of water to the evergreen shores on the farther side and over the vast extent of forests which extend scores and scores of miles beyond one's vision. . . . For all those who are destined to go there and labor, what years of industrial happiness I thought were in store for them. . . . [I] pictured their pleasant homes, their constant occupation the opportunities for pleasure by the ownership of row boats, sailing craft, and even motor boats, for these will be within the power of all concerned to have and own."[4]

In Truman's eyes, Conifer was the epitome of Edward Bellamy's capitalism of the future as described in his 1888 classic *Looking Backward*. Here were lumberjack Horatio Algers spawned in the north woods. Many a viewer saw the pastoral or, in this case, sylvan scene as a natural and important part of the middle landscape, rather than as a threat to the grandeur of the lakes, mountains, or the social order. Taming the forest was manifest destiny, a great romantic endeavor. Or so it seemed to Truman, whose experience of Conifer was made even more euphoric by the presence of many fellow Pennsylvanians. There was the mill-log scaler, and Joe Jones and his wife; "here too, I found in all the majesty of his wonderful mustache, William Ketzell, known in Brookville and . . . DuBois. Joe Jones is master of the band here, and Ketzell is drummer." Conifer seemed a perfect place.

But not all was grand and glorious in the North Country. Truman's vision of a logging utopia might well have been shaken had he heard that there was crime among the pines. "Dear Father," Clyde Sykes wrote on October 12, 1920, "our Cranberry Lake office was entered by burglars last night and one of the safes blown open and between $3,000.00 and $3,500.00 was taken." The state police had been called, but "we have no clue as to who did the job." Since their insurance did not cover money stolen from the paymaster, Clyde wrote, "we are probably the losers in the case." There had, however, been an interesting development. Ferris Meigs had had his car stolen at Tupper Lake "the same night that our safe was robbed." The police found Meigs' car "wrecked over near Boonville and one man was killed." The three other men with him "took to the woods" and escaped. Circumstances led the "State police to connect this up with the fact that a car ran through Cranberry Lake when the robbery took place and went away again."

E. B. Goslin soused, Camp No. 2, Kildare, 1912.

Visitors to Conifer arrived and departed by way of Childwold Station where the Grasse River Railroad met the New York Central.

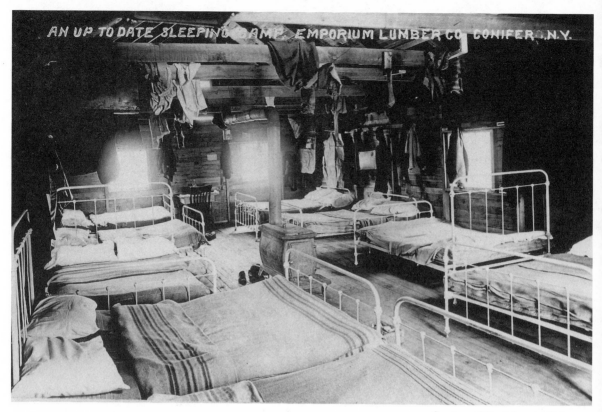

Up-to-date sleeping quarters at the Emporium Forestry Company in Conifer, New York. Postcard by H. M. Beach.

Alfred Truman thought Sykes' band mill at Cranberry Lake looked on a particularly pleasing prospect. Photograph taken in 1925.

Five days later, Clyde Sykes went to Cranberry Lake to check on the mill and discovered "that the experts on finger prints have taken pictures of the safe and other finger print marks around the office." He was content "that everything is being done that can be aside from our employing a private detective [which] seems unnecessary to me." William Turner, Emporium's treasurer, had met with the chief of police, the coroner from Boonville and a police detective in Utica and learned that

> " . . . Joe Spear was the dead man's brother. . . . I think the coroner thought that he knew something about the safe blowing but he did not have evidence enough to hold him. Now since you say that Joe was seen in Tupper Lake the night of the robbery and in company with a couple of other fellows it looks mighty suspicious."[5]

Although there was a good bit of information, nothing much was happening. Turner reported to Sykes " . . . that there did not seem to be any cooperation of the officers in St. Lawrence County with them here. . . . It seems to the writer that possibly our Company should offer a reward of something like $500 in order to put some 'pep' into the thing." Turner also wrote to George H. Bowers, Esq. of Canton that he had seen

> " . . . the County Treasurer of Oneida County today and they advise that they received your letter and would hold the funds until an investigation could be made. We also had a conference with the Chief of Police, who is holding the $964 that was found on James Walsh, one of the party in the auto wreck at Boonville. . . . He states that the attorney for the defendant will likely make a demand for this money in order to get funds to defend Walsh."[6]

The case was not solved by early November, much to the annoyance of W. L. Sykes. "If the case is so carelessly handled as the papers indicate the robbers may get away and not be punished." With the situation about the same as it was when the robbery occurred, what was to prevent "the same fellows" from coming back and doing "the stunt over again at Conifer?" When W. L. talked to

> " . . . John Riley and Mr. Owen at the Grasse River Club they indicated they were following the case up as best they could, . . . but the longer it goes the less money we are liable to get, for if they allow the robbers to run at large after having it for a time, it will not take long before they hide or dispose of the money so if they are caught later the money will have disappeared."[7]

Nothing else pertaining to the robbery appears in the company correspondence—the case apparently went unsolved.

If the number of felonies was modestly low, the misdemeanors were not. Drinking and fighting, if one is to believe the anecdotal histories of Adirondack logging, were major recreational pastimes among those who are now most frequently called the old-time lumberjacks. Even if no other record survived other than that of the sky pilot missionaries who visited the camps—and who found drinking an anathema—it is safe to say that appreciable amounts of liquor were consumed and violent disagreements were not unknown. The late William Marleau in his *Big Moose Station* vividly recalled—and perhaps embellished—an altercation that took place at Big Moose:

> "What really happened in the fight was this. Strife hired a large group of Russians, Poles and French Canadians to cut the pulp. He housed them in separate camps because they didn't get along in mixed groups. About twenty Poles were out at the hotel drinking and one of them wanted to fight somebody. They finally provoked an equally big Canadian to fight but a lot of hard words were used before the actual fight took place.
>
> The Canadian knocked the Pole out with two punches and then all the the other Poles jumped in. It was eighteen to one until the Canadian's little five foot six inch partner pitched in to help him. By that time, the Canadian had three more Poles lying on the ground. The Little Canadian was knocked down. As he started to get up, he was kicked in the face with a caulked shoe driving his eye way back into his head and knocked him out. Sheer weight of numbers got the big Canadian down and out. Then, lumberjack style, they put the boots to him. Raking his head and body with sweeping kicks so that the caulks on the boots would slash and rip."[8]

This was pretty vicious stuff which may have been caused by the diverse ethnic backgrounds—Russian, Poles and French Canadians—where natural enmities were heightened by alcohol. Violence, however, may not always have been the rule. The Rev. Frank Reed pointed out that

> "Some have described the old-time lumberjack as one who was prone to fight. . . . The sky pilot spent several thousand evenings in bunk-houses and never saw a fight. There was seldom an argument. These men spent their energies in long hours of labor and useful effort. Why would they argue and fight?"[9]

Outside the bunkhouse it was a different matter. Long periods of isolation contributed to hard drinking and short fuses, particularly, it seemed, around Tupper Lake. "Old-time lumberjacks some of whom lived in Tupper Lake but many of whom made their homes in the camps . . . came to town only at Christmas time and at the end of the log haul in mid-March. . . ." Reed pointed out that

> " . . . the lumberjack was a great commercial opportunity and little more. Many of the men . . . would tell the bartender to set up drinks for the house. After a state of intoxication had overwhelmed the lumberjack he was often relieved of his roll of bills. 'Treating the house' and 'rolling' soon exhausted his hard earned money. He was then ready for another trip back to hard labor in the forest."[10]

Stories and ballads often perpetuated the mean and brutal side of camp life. At Blue Mountain Lake, Billy Mitchell was:

> As mean a damn man as ye ever did see
> He'd lay round the shanty from mornings 'til night
> If a man said a word he was ready to fight.
> One morning before dawn Jim Lou got mad
> and knocked hell out of Mitchell
> and the boys was all glad.[11]

Romeo Arsenault's recollections of his days as a lumberjack give a marvelous picture of what went on when the logging season ended. His daughter writes, "The men left the camps and headed for civilization, . . . in Romeo's case, Tupper Lake. There the men pursued a variety of activities—most of which concerned women and/or alcohol. Despite their wild reputations the lumberjacks were generally regarded to be gentlemen and contributed much to the economics of the towns and cities they visited."[12]

Robert Bethke insightfully states that most owners and bosses were totally against drinking; that "No woods boss could afford alcohol-induced" friction in his work crews. According to Herbert Keith,

> " . . . the Rich Lumber Company prohibited the sale of intoxicating liquor on their lands in Township 15, . . . when . . . the company sold most of its holdings . . . the deed carried the provision: 'The party of the second part . . . shall not at any time manufacture or sell, as beverage, any intoxicating liquor nor permit the same to be done on the premises hereby conveyed.' "

By January 1919, "the prohibition law [18th amendment] became effective for the whole country. It is questionable that any serious deprivation ensued under either local regulation or federal law."[13]

Ferris Meigs described the attitude toward drinking in his company town:

"Santa Clara was in many respects a typical frontier town, except that, as all the property was owned by the Lumber Company, drinking places were prohibited. Not so at St. Regis Falls—six miles away. There, more than one hotel sold hard, (very hard) liquor, and saloons flourished. But here were many good citizens who worked to better conditions and outlaw whiskey. For years, elections were held. 'Local Option' was then the law, and finally local prohibition won."[14]

Even before the passage of the Volstead Act in 1920, the Prohibition Party in the North Country had been hard at work trying to achieve "the complete overthrow of the liquor traffic." In a letter from Olin S. Bishop, chairman of the New York State Prohibition Committee, to W. L. Sykes, the pitch was made that a financial contribution to support Prohibition candidates Hanly and Landrith would "bring about conditions for the betterment of your men as well as mankind in general." In the Sykes family, the Prohibitionists found strong supporters. They were ardent Methodists and teetotallers, anxious to stamp out Old Demon Rum and all of his works.

The concern over drinking gave life to politics in general, and clues to the politics of logging company owners. Clyde Sykes wrote the chairman of the St. Lawrence County Republican Committee in October 1919:

"It is with difficulty that we can get two Democrats to serve on our election board, our whole community being Republican. Quite a number of our people have been voting the Prohibition ticket. . . . We have 167 voters registered for election and practically all of them I think will enroll as Republicans."[15]

There were plenty of drinkers, if not Democrats, to stamp out.

Illicit booze was everywhere. It was destined to get worse as the antidrink crusaders took up their hatchets in earnest. But the bootleggers were very clever and, in at least one case, used a knowledge of logging to their best advantage. The *Watertown Daily Standard*, published in Gouverneur in July 1920, tells the story. Bootleggers were moving booze from Canada into the United States only to have their method revealed near Emoryville, when a load of pulpwood arrived at the

Oswegatchie paper mill

"... and it was discovered that the logs had been bored and the cavities filled with bottles of gin. The logs upon being inspected carefully revealed the presence of about 400 quarts of this liquor, according to the reports received here. The openings of the borings were skillfully concealed and the logs were as innocent looking as if nothing but mere wood."[16]

The hounds of righteousness in the form of the New York Civic League were on the scent, determined to ferret out "the name of any person who is seen intoxicated in your town or in any other town in the state of New York." Quick to cooperate, the owners of the Emporium Forestry Company mailed off a "list of suspects who are supposed to be bringing in liquor" at Conifer and Cranberry Lake in October 1920. Names were given and accusations made. Sherman Jones was "known to be a large dealer in liquor and ... large amounts are consumed in Cranberry Lake and vicinity." At Conifer, five people were cited for either bringing in liquor or dealing in booze. One person identified to the Civic League was "sick in the Homeopathic Hospital in Utica with typhoid fever." The company assured the League that "if we can get any additional information we will pass it along to you" and, as an afterthought, added the name of George LeClair of Conifer. Then, with a bit of guilt and perhaps self-protection, the informer added a note in longhand: "All I know about the above names is heresay, but the booze has been strong enough." One wonders if this last revelation was also by hearsay.

Action was not fast enough to please Sykes. On October 19, 1920, he chided the Civic League for not answering his earlier letters. He went on to say:

"I hear remarks to the effect that there is more liquor now than before the days of prohibition. ... We find that our woodsmen whenever they go to Tupper Lake are able to return with all the liquor they want, both in bottles and inside themselves. Recently I have witnessed a number of them carrying bottles and treating others and some of them were so intoxicated they could not walk."[17]

To get whiskey drinking out of the woods was an impossible task. Getting strong drink out of Tupper Lake was an even more formidable one. The federal Prohibition agent, William N. Allen, Jr., was having a tough time tracking down offenders, but the Civic League was "having investigations made at Tupper Lake in order to secure evidence against the smugglers and the boot-leggers, that are in business at that town, and who furnish the liquors, in our opinion, for Conifer, Cranberry Lake, Long Lake, Indian Lake and Newcomb."[18]

Illegal drinking was not confined to any one part of the mountains. In October 1924, federal agents raided Beaver River in an attempt "to check the notorious flow of whiskey among the lumberjacks . . . cutting timber there for the St. Regis Paper Company of Watertown." What they found was reported in the Utica newspaper, with all the overtones of a melodrama. When the agents got to the lumber camps, they found

> " . . . several hundred French Canadian huskies living in tumble down shacks or some of them with the bare ground for a bed and the sky for a roof. Beaver River didn't look like the Twentieth Century and New York State. And least of all did it resemble the new era of prohibition. The two objectives of the flying squadron were a cafe . . . and a hotel. Both were believed to be the chief source of liquor supply for the lumberjacks."

In addition to the liquor, there was a female presence to contend with, a Mrs. Smith by name, who was known as Jesse, the queen of the camp. It seemed that she "always has her pony nearby and her six shooter is fastened to her belt. . . . The prohibition men let her alone. They didn't even ask if she had a permit to carry the gun. They feared she might have shown them, but not in the usual way."[19]

If the men were making names for themselves in the camps and taverns, blowing off steam with the help of whiskey, their families were frequently disturbing the peace without it. Neighbors and their children got into altercations over a multitude of real and imagined grievances, and it seemed always that the aggrieved appealed to the boss for help. In 1920, a mother told Clyde Sykes that

> "I am writing you a few lines to see if you will furnish us another house or else see what you can do about making some of the nabors shut there mouths. There are a few Catect families up here that just abuse me. I can't go on the porch without they call us prodeson sun bitches and langue that I won't repeat. . . . They put up there children to fight with mine, and then they get out and call names, I have try every way I know how to use them nice but it's impossible. . . . There is a girl up here fourteen years old pounds my little boy only four and my baby only two years. . . . They steal there play things off the steps, I've got so all to pieces that I dont feel like showing myself. Just stay

at home and cry."

She was not the only one to complain that summer.

> " . . . neibors on the upper part of this street would like to lieve in peace, without being anoyed and insulted every few days by a family here by the name of Mrs. Day and her two oldest children. . . . There ought to be a way to protect people from being insulted by minors as well as old ones."[20]

Consider the familiar-sounding difficulty that another mother was having with a little boy named Kenneth. In the winter of 1935, she complained

> " . . . it seems that Kenneth can't mind his own business. He picks on Minnie continually. . . . I can't stand this continual coming home ever day with Minnie crying. Today she came home with her mouth bleeding where Kenneth hit her. I wouldn't mind if Minnie was a boy she could pound him back but you know how boys has the upper hand of a girl."[21]

It appears that neither loggers nor their families drank any more or less or fought any more frequently than workers in a coal-patch village in Pennsylvania or in a steel town along the Ohio River. Nor were references and slurs involving another person's ethnic origins and religious preference heard more frequently in the woods than in the mill towns. Only time has quieted such affronts. They now lie shallowly below the surface, no longer routine discourse across back porch railings or on the wooden sidewalks of company towns.

If the role of alcohol was traditional and its presence pervasive, the role of religion in the lumber camps was at best minimal. It continued to be despite the efforts of a group of dedicated woods missionaries or "sky pilots" such as Aaron Maddox, Frank Reed, Clarence Mason and others. In 1915, Aaron Maddox was quite frank and realistic about this when he wrote

> "The Woodsmen are of all sorts and conditions, all degrees of moral development and intelligence, and of several religions or none at all. One foreman, in giving permission for a service, said he did not think religion troubled his men much. . . . The camp service is the only religious service many of them ever see, and a sermon to them is a desirable novelty."

Occasionally, too much religion could be an obstacle to hiring a man or, at least, it gave a prospective employer cause for thought. In one case, a man was given a bad recommendation because he "is very religious and at present is very much taken up with it but if he could get away from where he is now that could be stopped. I believe in religion but not this way, The Holy Rollers."[22]

Nevertheless, in 1915, the American Bible Society distributed the scriptures around the North Country camps printed in at least ten different languages. Maddox recalled a missionary who "had given a young Italian a gospel and the next day as he was walking along the state road to a lumber camp, the Italian met him and proudly holding up the Gospel said, 'me hava him.' " To get to the 150 or more camps spread through the mountains was a feat in itself. Men recalled that "several times a year a preacher came to visit the jacks, who called him 'the Sky Pilot' and a priest would hold services nearby on Sundays, if he could find a place." All of this, of course, if it did not interfere with the pack peddler's Sunday visit or a poker game.

The logging villages or, more specifically, the company towns frequently had a resident minister. At Conifer, church, state and business were not separated. Emporium employed over 280 persons and needed not only the services of a physician in residence (which they had) but also a resident minister who was to see to the general spiritual condition of the workers and their families if not directly to the Christian character and conduct of the business. The minister held services in the basement of the public school (which received county money) and looked to the company and its men for his succor. In April 1919, W. Clyde Sykes needed "a minister for Conifer." A deeply motivated Methodist, Sykes turned to the Northern New York Conference at Fulton for help. He was quite specific about what he was looking for. He told Dr. E. H. Joy and Bishop William Burt that he wanted

> " . . . a man's man who could meet all types. A real lumberjack preacher of a type of man who would be a good Y.M.C.A. worker in an army camp, would probably fit very well here. We really need a stronger mixer and pastor rather than a preacher. . . . we have been able to raise the funds so easily from year to year that it seems to me that we can better this if we get a man who will appeal to the lumbermen. . . . These lumbermen usually make pretty good money and I believe will help us in our work financially. . . . I believe that a little different type of man would appeal better to the particular element I have already referred to."[23]

Family feuds and spats were not unknown in industrial villages and Conifer was no exception. Photographer H. M. Beach was commissioned by W. L. Sykes to document company operations and life in 1917.

The Methodist Episcopal Sunday School at Conifer, Children's Day, June 24, 1917. Postcard by H. M. Beach.

Aaron Maddox began his Adirondack ministry in 1914 and for twenty-five years preached the word of God in the lumbercamps. This photograph was probably taken in 1914.

St. Paul's Roman Catholic Church at Piercefield, New York. The majority of loggers in the North Country were nominally Roman Catholics.

Diplomatic, yes, but barely. No one could miss the point, not even a Methodist Bishop. Namby-pambies were not going to have much success preaching God's Word in the environs of a logging camp or village.

John Stock, long-time superintendent and resident of Conifer, recalled that the village was very supportive of the Conifer charge.

> "The church, Methodist, was an adjunct of the Tupper Lake charge. At the peak occupancy of the hamlet, there was a resident minister who lived in the parsonage. There was an occasional 'lady preacher' who lived at the Hotel. This was the residence of the unmarried teachers. The Hotel (always capitalized and with the emphasis on the first syllable) never failed to feature a chicken dinner on Sunday, and this could well be the treat of the week."[24]

Alfred T. Truman had commented in 1917 that a minister at Conifer got paid as much there as for "preaching in the larger population centers." In 1912, W. Clyde Sykes had written to A. J. Fields, superintendent of schools at Winthrop, about starting a public school at Conifer for the village's children, twenty of whom were of school age. It was the consensus, confided Sykes, "that they would like a protestant teacher." Such are the parameters of social change and the law of the land between 1912 and the present day.

The denominational profile of the woods worker is difficult to determine accurately since churches were in the towns and, despite the best efforts of the various "mission bands," services of any description were infrequent in the logging camps. In the very early 1950s, eighty-two percent of the lumberjacks considered themselves Roman Catholic, mostly because of the prevalence of French-Canadian and Irish woodsmen in the Adirondacks. Thirteen percent were Protestants and five percent were agnostics. This latter figure was probably much higher simply because of the great number of fallen-away communicants of all denominations who, because of their isolation, had had little or no contact with the more formal conduct of religious services and practice.

Finally, as with almost every other aspect of Adirondack life, the coming of the automobile had its effect on organized religion in the remote areas of the North Woods. Comparing the first experiences of his woods ministry to that of his full-time work which began in 1938, Frank Reed was quick to note what a difference the car had made in changing his routines. He recalled that

> " . . . he had served camps in specific areas such as the southwestern or

northern Adirondacks in the early years and in later camp visits, he discovered that his parish now included the entire Adirondacks, the Tug Hill area west of the Adirondacks and the John E. Johnston operations in Vermont. . . . The coverage of this broader area was made possible by the fact that some new roads had been built and all roads were plowed in winter so one could make fuller use of automobile transportation. The sky pilot might have a hike of three or twenty miles to camp from the nearest highway, but he could travel to the general area by car all seasons of the year. This eliminated the necessity of travelling all winter on snowshoes as Clarence Mason had done in earlier years."[25]

Other routines also changed and utopia was never the same again. In 1941, the United States went to war. The lumberjack and woods worker went, too. Although his fighting, drinking and religious propensities might be questioned, there was little doubt about his patriotism. One example will suffice. At the beginning of the New Year, 1943, Corporal George Parrotte was in North Africa, where on November 8, 1942, American forces had landed at Casablanca, Oran and Algiers. He wrote home to Mr. and Mrs. Clyde Sykes at Conifer in the February respite before the Battle of the Kasserine Pass. First, he wanted to thank everyone there who had sent him a package although he had not yet received it. Also he wanted everyone to know that the weather had been pretty good except for a little rain, but it was "nothing like the weather at Conifer." Then came the G.I.'s usual understatement: "We are having a pretty rough life here," but it was alright, since he was

> " . . . sure we will never regret the part that we are doing to keep the folks back home and the rest of the world free from the chains of the Axis forces. We are fighting for the freedom that the Axis powers never knew and know that in the end with God's help and our struggle that we will in the end win. Our valiant boys are over here giving their lives for the good old U.S.A. and the Axis forces are fighting against the most powerful Army, Navy & Marine force the world has ever seen and these boys bear the name of an American."[26]

Corporal Parrotte's letter tells us more about the North Country and its people than all the folk songs and ballads and historical essays ever written or sung.

CHAPTER FIVE

The Hazards of Woods Work

"The lumberer's life in the forest, through long, cold winters . . . , is one of great hardship and peril."

—*Horace Greeley*, 1872

Accidents have been mentioned in every medium dealing with the history of logging. Descriptions of the industry never failed to mention its high-risk aspects; newspapers and the loggers themselves, in songs and ballads, often recalled the tremendous excitement and danger of their work. Take Tebo, for example, who was driving logs on the Raquette River:

It was on Monday morning
About the hour of ten,

a drive-boss named Thomas routed out his crew to break a log jam.

The logs were piled up mountain high,
The waters swift and strong,
To wash away poor Tebo
And the log that he was on

Hickey, a young man from around Saranac, tried to save poor Tebo.

The water would roll over them;
He was forced to let him go;

They found his drowned body.
In the Raquette River - O.

Tebo had been an older fellow who had been on many a log drive when he went under on the sixth of May. They did not see him again until the tenth, when—

They found his drained body
And laid it in the clay.

Tebo was dead; left behind were his widow and five small children. There were no pensions, no accident insurance, nothing. Only his drive-mates were still there and

A collection was made by all of them;
Each man his share did pay,
To feed and clothe the orphans
Left behind that day.[1]

The river drives were not the only source of great danger and the cause of injury and death among woodsmen. There were hazards galore just waiting to trap the luckless, the careless and the unskilled. Accidents in the woods and mills were commonplace and, before the era of work-men's compensation, the burden of being maimed or killed on the job accrued to the worker. In New York State, before 1910, the accident victim often received little assistance or sympathy from a boss or owner, while the threat or presence of an epidemic disease usually brought prompt response, particularly when the work force was threatened and the public frightened.

Businessmen, during the first two decades of the twentieth century, were resentful of a rising number of anti-trust actions, federal controls imposed by World War I, and those forces in the country who campaigned for better labor conditions—hours, wages, benefits, and healthful workplace environments. "So much is being done to benefit every class of people but the business man," complained W. L. Sykes of the Emporium Forestry Company in 1919. The businessman

" . . . takes risks and puts in 15 hours a day in order that he may give employment to a lot of people who are constantly wearing his life out because they want 8 hours a day at larger pay than they get for 10 hours. . . . You know we are over-burdened with commissioners and laws that prevent a man from doing business."[2]

Social Darwinism cloaked in the respectability of Christian morality made it easy for many to close their eyes to the real needs of the working man and his family. The fact was that many persons needed help and protection from the unrestrained exercise of power on the part of the businessman and his friends. The belief that the weak got hurt and the strong survived was ameliorated often only by an owner's awareness that it was in his own self-interest to keep his work force at full strength. One way was to provide minimal accident compensation for employees hurt on the job, but even this was slow to gain acceptance.

In 1920, W. Clyde Sykes, in response to an inquiry from"The Institute for Crippled and Disabled Men" located in New York City, clearly suggested the tenor of the times. The Institute wished to have information on a Mr. E. H_____. Sykes told the writer everything he wanted to know about E. H_____, including the most personal aspects of his medical history. He wrote that

> "H____ took a contract for the getting out of pulpwood for our company. . . . He paid no attention to business, became injured and then tried to make himself out an employee instead of a contractor and has employed lawyers on several occasions to try to force us to pay him money not due. He has condemned our physician, whom we know to be a very capable man, because of the fact that his flesh wound in his knee became infected thru his own carelessness and resulted in amputation being necessary. The infection I believe was a direct result of his own carelessness aided by the fact that he has syphilis, which prevented the wound from healing as it should have. . . ."[3]

Sykes may have had sympathy for the man because of the loss of his leg, but that was where his sensitivity, if any, stopped. All he recommended for a man who, in his opinion, was an unreliable, untruthful, one-legged syphilitic was that because of H____'s "experience in the woods" he was qualified "to sharpen saws and axes and perhaps sharpen all kinds of tools." Such responses were not unusual. In the years between the first passage and final adoption of a workmen's compensation law, an injured worker had few places where he could find help.

In 1912, while the new state compensation law was in limbo in the courts, an injured man was informed that although his employer regretted "extremely" the heavy damage that had been done to his hand, the Emporium Forestry Company would make no settlement. Furthermore, he was told "that our . . . Company carries a protective policy which authorizes them to pay the bills and other necessary expenses for the first twenty-four hours of treatment after the man is injured, and after that time the matter is entirely out of our hands." One can only wonder where the woodsman was to find help. A hand seemed minor compared to an eye injury incurred at Conifer in the lath mill. "The injured man was taken to the Montreal hospital on the evening train. The left eye was completely destroyed and the right eye might be seriously affected." Twenty-four hours' coverage and the inference that it must have been carelessness, since the "mill is equipped with all the safety devices known," were not a very positive prognosis for the injured man, but change was in the air for men like these and others.

In 1910, New York had become the first state in the Union to pass compulsory accident insurance legislation due mainly to the Wainwright Commission's investigative report to the state legislature. Unfortunately, the following year this first Workmen's Compensation Act was promptly declared unconstitutional. The law was passed again in 1913; however, it provided for direct settlement between owners and employees, a proviso which constantly worked to the disadvantage of the latter. In 1919, under pressure from Governor Al Smith, the law reverted to its original concept. The state now would review all work-related accident claims through the Bureau of Workmen's Compensation, an agency of the State Industrial Commission. Furthermore, all injuries were to be recorded and reported. The language was very clear.

> "Every employer shall keep a record of all injuries, fatal or otherwise, received by his employees in the course of their employment. . . . An employer who refuses or neglects to make a report as required by this section shall be guilty of a misdemeanor, punishable by a fine of not more than five hundred dollars."[4]

From 1919 forward, accident insurance periodically improved. Monetary awards for rated injuries and disabilities increased from fifteen to twenty-five dollars weekly; administration improved; a state insurance fund became operational; a list of hazardous jobs was extended to include those that exposed workers to the risks of occupational diseases. With all of this came a greater intrusion of bureaucracy including increasingly complicated forms and an expanded role for the private insurance carriers. Large operations such as the Emporium Forestry Company carried accident liability policies. Emporium's coverage in the early years was with the Lumber Mutual Casualty Insurance Company of New York and the Travelers; not surprisingly, W. L. Sykes, president of Emporium, was a member of the board of directors

WATCH OUT FOR FALLING LIMBS

THREE MEN HAVE BEEN KILLED RECENTLY
YOU COULD BE NEXT

Courtesy of The Adirondack Museum

American Pulpwood Association Safety Poster No. 5, 1952. This series of twelve posters was commissioned in 1952 and drawn by Dill.

The river drive was perhaps the most dangerous aspect of an otherwise very hazardous industry. This wood engraving by Harry Fenn entitled "Clearing a Jam, Great Falls of the Ausable" was published in 1874 by D. Appleton and Co.

Disabling injuries did not always preclude men from returning to the woods.

Courtesy of The Adirondack Museum

American Pulpwood Association Safety Poster No. 1.

STAND TO ONE SIDE WHEN TREE IS FALLING
WATCH FOR KICKBACKS

Courtesy of The Adirondack Museum

THE SAFE WAY
TO CUT SPRING POLES

American Pulpwood Association Safety Poster No. 3.

Courtesy of The Adirondack Museum

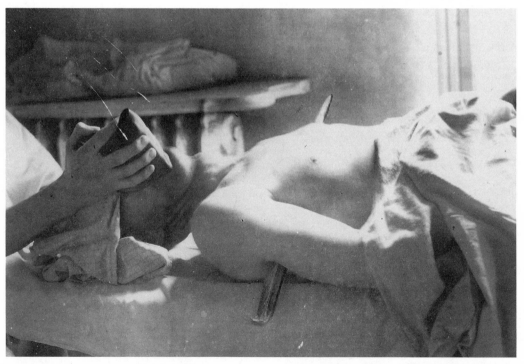

Courtesy of The Adirondack Museum

The injury to edgerman George Lanz of Forestport on June 14, 1906 at the Pullman Mill in Thendara, New York was documented photographically and in circus-like broadsides. His recovery seemed to be a minor miracle.

of Lumber Mutual.

The new law, in addition to its humanitarian virtues, had another positive effect: it recorded the number and variety of accidents which occurred in the work force. The Emporium records, in particular, give insight into a major Adirondack logging and saw milling concern which, between the two World Wars, employed an average of 285 persons at both Conifer and Cranberry Lake. The company reported to the Deputy Commissioner of Labor in 1919: "We have a resident physician, who has a fully equipped office, including an operating room." No doubt this helped to keep Lumber Mutual's rates down. It also helped in moving compensation cases through the state rating board since they, too, had looked into "our facilities in taking care of injuries" and found "ample evidence that we could take care of a cut in a man's foot." A "cut" foot had occurred in April 1918, and had resulted in the amputation of a man's little toe and also "the greater part of the metatarsal bone." The company, guarding its liability, was quick to point out to the deputy commissioner that this man's loss was due to the fact that "he was careless . . . and allowed his wound to become infected, and would not see our Doctor, although he was requested to return to the office for further treatment." One year later, after pushing his claim, the man received an award of $17.18 per week for thirty-five weeks, or a total of $572.16 as a result of a State Industrial Commission special hearing held at the Court House in Utica, on May 1, 1919.[5]

Historically, where there were railroads there were accidents, and the logging roads were no exception. In January 1918, the train master of the Grasse River Railroad reported: "We had a little accident today. It happened about 9:00 a.m. One car of pulp-wood, car of poles and a cargo of coal got away from Frazer at Childwold Station." Poor Frazer had forgotten to have the safety switch aligned properly and "the cars run down and jumped the track . . . and wrecked the three cars rather bad." Saving the best news for last, the train master added: "No one was hurt." For his carelessness, Frazer was disqualified as a regular conductor for six months and reduced to the status of an "extra conductor or brakeman, wages to be .32 per hour." He was also forbidden "to smoke in the yard (lumber) and is to collect all fares." (It was found he was passing people without authority.)[6]

Almost a year later, a 41-year-old worker from Cranberry Lake was forced to jump from a run-away portion of a log train when a coupling broke on a car. He was lucky and only bruised his right heel and hip; however, it was another one of those "bruises" which laid a man off for two weeks. Another man was coupling log cars in the Conifer yards in the summer of 1920 when his right hand got caught between the two couplers badly crushing his little finger. It had to be amputated by Dr. Cohen who saw him almost immediately after the accident.

In the woods, the usual accidents continued to happen. Falls and slips, occasioned by bad weather, rough terrain, or rotten logs; falling tree limbs and rolling or sliding logs were all causes of injuries to loggers. For example, a 60-year-old woodsman working out of Conifer in June 1919, "stepped on a rotten log and fell, severely bruising his left leg. He was out of work for a week and received $15.00 compensation for his time without pay." The man could ill-afford to lose his usual earnings of $3.15 per day since, as the company explained, he was considerably in arrears with his store account. "They haven't paid anything on this account since October 4th, 1919," wrote Victor Noelk, assistant paymaster, "and unless it is taken care of at once you know we cannot afford to let them continue to have the house and not get any rent for same."

Between 1921 and the 1930s, the accident reports continued to pile up in the company's files. With little exception, the nature of the injuries were similar to those mentioned, occurring in the woods, in the mills, and around the railroad and tramways. But fatal injury was not unheard of: on May 19, 1927, George W. Sykes reported the death of a worker to the Lumber Mutual Casualty Insurance Company. Sykes wrote that M____ "was not our employee . . . but was cutting wood on our land for another party." On the afternoon of May 18, "he attempted to get on our log train . . . missed his footing and fell and was rolled under the train and died a short time later. The train was running about 10 miles per hour." Henry Dean saw the accident take place. He gave a sworn statement as follows:

"As the log train was proceeding about 150 yards above Tate's camp, [M____] who was standing on the East side of the track made an attempt to get on the Caboose by placing both hands on the grab irons and trying to board the train while it was in motion. He carried a small pasteboard box in his hand about a foot square. This box he had in his right hand.

I was sitting on the top step of the caboose. His left hand slipped from the grab iron first, and as it did I tried to reach him and pull him on but he stumbled and fell. The boxing on the following car hit him first. I jumped from the train as soon as possible and flagged them, but before they could stop he had been rolled over a number of times and his head finally struck the rail and the wheels on the second car struck his head."[7]

Injury to older men was a common occurrence, moreso because World Wars I and II had called many young men to service.

Occasionally, a logging accident almost instantly became folklore. Such was the case of George Lanz who in 1906 worked at the Pullman Brothers sawmill in Forestport. Lanz, from Forestport, was an edgerman and one day lifted a piece of spruce which was stuck on the saw. The Rev. Frank Reed describes the incident as he heard it from the Old Forge doctor who had treated Lanz. Reed recounts that as the piece of edging came free

" . . . the swiftly-revolving saw caught it again and sent it like a bolt of lightning. The thirteen-foot edging pierced Mr. Lanz's chest and came through on the right side of his back, also piercing his right arm. Members of the mill crew carefully sawed both ends of the thirteen-foot piece so Mr. Lanz could ride in the baggage car. He was treated by Dr. Nelson who accompanied him on the train to St. Elizabeth's Hospital in Utica. After careful examination, Dr. Hyland, a prominent surgeon on the hospital staff, decided to remove the edging through the back and proceeded to do so. George Lanz recovered and had many useful years of service."[8]

Not only has the verbal account survived but so has a photograph which was later rendered as a tabloid-like painting showing poor Lanz, spruce and all, through his arm and chest about to undergo the operation that saved his life. Dr. Hyland's sixty-page report of Lanz's hospitalization survives as well, all in the Adirondack Museum collections.

The variety of accidents and their degree of seriousness never ceases to amaze those who think of logging as little more than cutting down trees in the sylvan splendor of the mountains and lakes.

Some reports conjure images which are almost humorous had not the narrowness of an escape or just plain luck intervened to prevent real harm to a worn-out logger. It seems that E. L____, age 55 and of Brandreth Lake, in February 1950, stopped to rest for the night, smoked a cigarette, fell asleep and set the mattress on fire. *The Lumber Camp News* reported

" . . . according to State Police of the Long Lake detail, who investigated, E. L____ was returning to the Finch Pruyn lumber camp about eight miles south of Long Lake, where he is employed, and stopped to sleep in an empty bunkhouse along the road. The fire was discovered by the camp foreman when he stopped for an axe to clear away fallen trees which blocked the road to the logging camp. Dr. Morrison J. Hosley of Long Lake treated E. L____'s burns and he was removed to the hospital in the Finch Pruyn ambulance. His condition is not serious.[9]

Nearly eight months after E. L____ almost torched himself, he was involved in another accident. This time luck was not present, particularly for "Big John," age 60 who was struck in the head by a falling limb from a huge birch which he and E. L____ had just cut down. The result was fatal; Big John was dead and E. L____ narrowly escaped.

They died young and old from the dangers of the woods and frequently it seemed as if the luck of the draw determined who survived and who did not. The woods, mills and railroads, all integral parts of the logging experience, produced a steady, almost unending list of casualties among workers. "Widow makers," limbs which break off one tree and hang on another, still kill people, as do "fool-killers," young trees or saplings caught and bent over making them into deadly coiled springs. In 1949, *The Lumber Camp News* compared woods-related accidents of earlier days with the modern era of logging and concluded that "old-time lumbering was probably twice as dangerous as operations are today. . . . But old-timers were more experienced. They knew how to handle themselves, so accidents weren't much more frequent than they are today."[10]

Was this assessment of the historic situation wishful thinking, or folklore? Or was it the apologia of a trade journal? Maybe it was a bit of all three. One thing, however, is clear. The woods and the ancillary mills were places where people got hurt, often severely. The major difference between the earlier days and more recent ones was that a victim's chances of survival had improved along with the level of medical care and insurance coverage. The best example of this is the case of a young woodsman paralyzed from the chest down by a tree which struck him across the spine near Newcomb on October 5, 1951. Unlike an earlier time, he was flown to Bellevue Medical Center from Saranac Lake—a trip paid for by his employer's insurance company.[11]

Between 1910, which saw the first vestiges of compensation coverage for on-the-job injury, and 1950, there had been progress in the woods. In the 1950s, the injured eye might well have been saved, and the leg healed with the syphilis arrested. If any aspect of logging strips away the aura of romance and folklore it is the incidence of pain, loss of limb and of life itself suffered by men while working at a back-breaking occupation where the nature of the workplace precluded many of the safety features found in factories in urban settings at comparable dates. Courage was needed to survive in the woods, and workers who labored in the Adirondacks had more than their share. Through the years, the logger was slowly and partially brought under the umbrella of worker's benefits; today logging is still considered one of the most hazardous of occupations by those who provide compensation insurance. Curiously, the woodsmen's hat can stand symbol for his advance into the age of worker's safety. The soft stocking cap or felt hat worn by the earlier chopper and sawyer disappeared and in its place came the ubiquitous hard hat of the industrial worker. Individuality may have been lost in the switch from soft hat to hard, but in the process perhaps a few lives were saved.

Accidents were not the only foe of the woodsman in the early days of Adirondack logging. Communicable disease was always present. This was particularly true when large numbers of men were crowded into logging camp bunk-houses, mess halls or boarding houses where sanitary conditions were frequently less than ideal.

Added to the difficulty of maintaining proper sanitation was the public belief that disease lurked in places where persons had been previously ill; together, these amounted to a sometimes severe problem for businessmen, from hotel owners to lumber barons. Typhoid fever—characterized by red rashes, high fever, bronchitis and intestinal bleeding—was a frequent visitor in many communities well into the twentieth century. Water was the most frequently identified vehicle of transmission and food, particularly milk, was a close second. Food handlers such as cooks and cooks-helpers carried the disease as did flies that spread the bacteria (*Salmonella typhosa*) from feces to food. The old doggerel:

> *The fly flew into the company store*
> *Lit on cheese, lit on the ham*
> *and cleaned himself up on the grocery man*

is a graphic reminder of one way that the disease was spread.

ALWAYS WALK ON UPHILL SIDE OF LOG
WHEN DRIVING HORSE

*American Pulpwood Association
Safety Poster No. 9.*
    Courtesy of The Adirondack Museum

GARDEZ VÔTRE ATTENTION À L'OUVRAGE
ET LE CROCHET DANS LE BOIS

*American Pulpwood Association
Safety Poster No. 10.*
    Courtesy of The Adirondack Museum

CARRY YOUR TOOLS
SAFELY

American Pulpwood Association
Safety Poster No. 6.
        Courtesy of The Adirondack Museum

BE SAFE...

KEEP IT

SHARP →
← TIGHT
SOUND

American Pulpwood Association
Safety Poster No. 2.
        Courtesy of The Adirondack Museum

CHECK YOUR AXE
EVERY DAY

PRECAUTION AGAINST INFLUENZA

Wash hands before each meal   Gargle throat with saline, (one fourth teaspoonful of common salt, 1 cup of water.) Cough and sneeze in your handkerchief Do not spit on the floor or side walk Eat pleanty of nourishing food Take pleanty of exercise in the open air   Sleep with window open.

How to recognize Flu.

The symptoms are fever, chills and a feeling of cold in the head.   Aching in the bones and joints may occur. There may be constipation or diarrhea.

Treatment.

KEEP YOUR HEAD.   TAKE CASTOR OIL.   GO TO BED.   CALL A DOCTOR.

Newcomb, N.Y., Feb. 5, 1920.

J. J. OWEN
Health Officer.

Courtesy of The Adirondack Museum

Communicable diseases like typhoid fever and influenza also threatened lumberjacks' health and lives. Board of Health broadside from Piercefield, New York c. 1920.

BOARD OF HEALTH

PIERCEFIELD, N. Y.

HOW TO PREVENT TYPHOID FEVER

TYPHOID GERMS

The germs are carried in the secretions and discharges from the human body, and in the majority of cases are transmitted to others through carelessness and lack of knowledge as to how the disease is carried to others.

A person does not have to be sick to give Typhoid Fever. We have people who are known as carriers and may never have had the disease and yet they are the dangerous ones.

PREVENTIONS

Food, in its raw state, is one of the main carriers or Typhoid germs. Therefore, all food should be cooked at least for 20 minutes, as food so prepared, will be free from the germs.

Do not use any food which has been exposed to flies before cooking, and see that flies do not have access to food at any time.

Upon using toilets, always wash hands thoroughly, and especially when you are going to handle food stuffs.

All toilets should be thoroughly screened against flies, as they are one of the most dreaded carriers of disease.

SWAT THE FLY and screen your windows and doors.

WATER is one of the common carriers of the Typhoid germ, but by boiling it 20 minutes it will be purified and rendered fit for drinking purposes.

MILK is a carrier of the Typhoid germs, through the contamination of flies, or the dirty hands of the dairyman. To sterilize milk, place bottle in vessel containing sufficient water to cover the bottle two-thirds of its height, and be sure to place some metal, such as nails or piece of chain, in bottom of kettle, setting the bottle on the nails or chain, to avoid cracking the bottle, and boil for 20 minutes. Keep mouth of bottle closed, to avoid contamination from flies.

THE TYPHOID VACCINE—Apply to your physician, or the health officer.

There is no danger incurred entering a house where there is a case of the disease, if the following precautions are followed:

DO NOT touch sick person.

DO NOT touch or handle dishes.

DO NOT come in contact with bedclothing.

DO NOT use same toilet.

DR. I. A. ALLEN,
Health Officer.

Courtesy of Warder Cadbury

Broadside from Board of Health, Newcomb, New York.

Typhoid fever in the Adirondacks was certainly not a rare occurrence. In both 1892 and 1900 thirty or forty cases of typhoid had been reported at Blue Mountain Lake and at the nearby Marion River Carry. Three years later several more cases were reported at Prospect House on the lake. In time, typhoid effectively put that hotel—a commanding, three-story structure—out of business. In 1906, there were still more cases at Blue Mountain Lake; by 1909, eighteen more had been sporadically reported, most at Camp Eagle Nest on the west end of the lake. Eventually the outbreak was traced to a carrier, Harry Williams, a night watchman. He received almost as much notoriety as had Typhoid Mary, first of the renowned carriers. In December 1910, *The New York Times* contributed to Williams' fame by referring to him as a "Walking Typhoid contributed to Williams' fame by referring to him as a "Walking Typhoid Factory," and suggested to its readers that there were probably as many as ten thousand unknown carriers in the United States. In 1916, a carrier at Francis P. Garvan's Kamp Kill Kare, about twenty miles from Blue Mountain Lake and Eagle Nest, caused another epidemic.[12]

On September 23, 1920, at Conifer, W. Clyde Sykes, assistant to the president of the Emporium Forestry Company, wrote to the quartermaster at U.S. Army Headquarters, Governor's Island. "We are having a typhoid epidemic and wish to procure Lister bags for the treatment of drinking water," an initiative prompted by the district health officer, Dr. I. A. Allen in Piercefield. Sykes got a fast reply, albeit a bureaucratic one, which referred him to the Field Medical Supply Depot at 21st and M. St., N.E. in Washington, D.C. to procure the water bags.

Alfred Truman, the Sykes' friend from Pennsylvania, wrote to them on September 22, 1920, that he was coming to Conifer for a visit. On the twenty-fifth, Clyde Sykes replied, "We are having a typhoid epidemic here and it may be that it will be wise for you to wait a few days longer before coming so as to make sure of conditions here. . . . " Truman did not come nor did things improve quickly at Conifer. On January 11, 1921, Clyde Sykes wrote to the company's president: "Dear Father . . . we have three new cases of typhoid in the past couple of weeks." He enclosed a letter he had written to Dr. Senftner, the state epidemiologist in Buffalo. Sykes explained:

> "It now appears that the local Health Officer and the State authorities have absolutely dropped us and it is up to us to stamp out this typhoid as best we can without any State or Town assistance. . . . I wish you would make a personal call on Dr. Senftner, whose office is

in the Ellicott Square, and without letting him know that we feel the
Department has dropped us see if you cannot get him to take further
interest in our matter. . . . Dr. Senftner himself advised me to see that
all our convalescents from typhoid were carefully examined to see if
they might be carriers and now is certainly the time to get this typhoid
situation cleared up or we will have a much worse time of it next
spring."[13]

Emporium was threatened by an epidemic, and alarmed by thoughts
of potential impact. Accidents presented one set of problems; typhoid
was quite another matter. While frustrated by the red tape, young Sykes
persevered and finally found Senftner prepared to be helpful. He wrote
to the doctor:

"I am rather discouraged over the typhoid situation in Conifer. I
have tried to arrange, as was suggested by you, to have all of the people
who have had typhoid tested out to see if they might be carriers. . . .
Meantime, I find we are having some more new cases of typhoid,
three having developed in the last couple of weeks, all in the boarding
house. . . . My thought is that with winter weather we are much less
liable to have typhoid than next spring when the flies return and the
ground does not have the blanket of snow over it which now prevails."[14]

Four days later Senftner replied to Sykes. He had "read with considerable interest the various statements" reported by Sykes and promised
he would "make every effort to come to Conifer not later than ten days
from today." Furthermore, he included with his letter a seventeen part
questionnaire which he wanted Dr. Allen, the district health officer, and
Dr. Cohen, Emporiums' physician, to fill out. In addition to the questionnaire, Senftner pointed out:

"There may have been some misunderstanding as to just what it
was that I desired, in the way of testing for carrier condition those who
had previously had typhoid fever. The idea that I wished to convey
was this, that whenever a secondary case, namely, a secondary case in
one and the same family, should occur that all those who may have
had typhoid during the present outbreak be requested to submit feces
and blood specimens to our laboratory in order that I might determine
whether they are carriers and perhaps a source of infection of the secondary case."[15]

Since October 10, there had been several new cases at the village—one in South Conifer, three in North Conifer, and three in the

boarding house. A suspected carrier had gone from the village in September 1920, but had returned for two days several weeks before Christmas. Of possibly greater importance, Henry Lafave and his wife both had contracted typhoid in the fall and both had had contact with the food supply. In fact, one freezer of ice cream had been served at the boarding house the night after Mrs. Lafave returned to work after her illness. Other than that, the only change in the boarding house food chain had been the hiring of Frank Baker around Christmastime as a choreboy. The water supply was checked and the main sources—a well in front of the Thomas house and the Childwold Station pump—had been examined in Albany and found safe. Other water, including that for the boarding house, had been boiled and a general order from the company to boil water continued in force throughout the village. With the onset of the disease, Dr. Cohen had begun to immunize workers. Even so, Louis Brownless, who had had two of his three immunization shots, contracted a mild case of typhoid. All persons who were sick were given the Widal blood test; all were found positive for typhoid. No fecal examinations were made. Some thirteen cases had been confirmed since early October. More individuals contracted the disease in November and December.

On January 19, 1921, Clyde Sykes acknowledged Senftner's letter. He made a point to tell him that he was pleased "to see the interest you are taking in the typhoid situation here." Finally, with testing and close supervision by the physicians and management, the number of cases lessened. Sykes again wrote Senftner telling him he was ignoring district health officer Allen's advice to turn on Conifer's reservoir water. He would keep it off "until I can hear from you and get your approval." The company wanted to make sure there would be no further outbreak, particularly

> " . . . now that we have located one carrier in the Conifer Boarding House I feel that our problem is at least partially met but the fact that this carrier had the disease during our epidemic does not account for the cases which occurred before she became a carrier. Right now at the spring of the year when the water is so high I do not want to take any chances that might in any way cause a recurrence of typhoid."[16]

April approached. Sykes continued to take precautions. As had the owners of Eagle Nest in Blue Mountain Lake several years earlier, he sought the advice and assistance of a sanitary engineer. He wrote that "it has not been proven that our typhoid fever was caused by water supply and in fact a carrier was located, but nevertheless it would seem wise to get experienced advice in the matter." He explained that "our location is approximately 100 miles north of Utica on the Adirondack Division of the New York Central. . . ." He asked James Caird, the engineer who was from Troy, if he could "spend a couple of days in the near future looking over our two small villages in the Adirondacks with the thought of making recommendations as to any changes which might be regarded as needed?"

This exchange virtually ended references to Emporium's typhoid epidemic except for an interesting postscript. On August 19, 1921, the company received a letter from Francis Barry Cantwell, an attorney at Saranac Lake representing a Mr. James Hulse of Rome. Cantwell stated that

> " . . . in December 1920 while working in your employ as a black-smith's helper at Conifer, N.Y. he [Hulse] contracted typhoid fever from the water supplied by your company. He says there was an epidemic of typhoid fever in Conifer at about the same time and that a large number of men besides himself came down with the disease and that an analysis of the water used there showed that it was infected with typhoid germs."[17]

Attorney Cantwell quickly outlined the debilitating aspects of typhoid fever and its effect on Hulse who, according to Cantwell, had been "laid up from January 7th to March 21st, 1921 before he could do any work and was confined in St. Elizabeth's Hospital from January 11th to March 11th, 1921 and incurred a hospital bill of $123.50. The attorney then let the company know that he had had plenty of experience handling such matters against some very powerful opposition. His intimidating reminder stated that he had "lately settled 23 different actions against the owners of Kamp Kill Kare near Racquette [sic] Lake when a settlement of $7,000.00 was made for all the cases which contracted typhoid in this epidemic." If this did not cause the Sykes to shake in their boots, then they had better be reminded of "a number of decisions recently holding cities and villages liable where there is typhoid in the water, and where the municipality had known in time to prevent the spread of the disease." Cantwell now made his pitch, writing that

> "I trust you would prefer to adjust this matter with Mr. Hulse for his lost time and his hospital bill rather than have him seek redress by a civil action for damages. . . . I think he can stand a fair chance of recovering something in an action for damages as his back is still weak

and he is unable to work as well as formerly. He is not disposed to be unreasonable but will compromise this matter as I have suggested by payment of his hospital bill of $123.50 and his wages for the time he was laid up."[18]

The Sykes did not blink. They immediately sent a copy of Cantwell's letter to their attorney and company trustee, the Honorable E. J. Jones, U.S. Congressman from the twenty-first district of Pennsylvania. "Cantwell's letter," said Sykes, "does not state the facts." He provided Jones with a scenario of the epidemic:

"Briefly, when typhoid fever broke out in this community, every precaution was used to prevent its spread. The state Epidemiologist has been here on several occasions and also other state officials. Our own doctor and the health officer have been right on the job and every recommendation and precaution that could be taken has been taken. Right in the beginning of the epidemic the water and milk were both suspected. We immediately advised everybody to boil the water and had the local milk supply examined."[19]

On August 30, Jones wrote two sentences to attorney Cantwell at Saranac Lake: "You are misinformed as to the facts in relation to the typhoid fever epidemic which occurred in this community in 1920 and 1921. We admit no liability whatever in connection with it."

Nothing further about the case is recorded in the company's correspondence, however, it clearly suggests an attitude about employer responsibility and liability in the aftermath of epidemic diseases. It spells out the impact on business. In the case of Hulse, the company had lost a blacksmith's services for over four months; this was far longer than the lost time occasioned by a fall, a cut or even a broken bone. With the threat of mass layoffs due to illness seriously interrupting operations and the possibility of subsequent civil suits, owners were quicker to apply preventive measures than to deal with the ramifications of cures. They were also very eager to avoid any public perception that they were running an operation or a business where unhealthy conditions or sickness prevailed.

On February 27, 1923, the *Watertown Daily Times* published an article picked up by *The Post Standard* in Syracuse and *The Tupper Lake Herald*. It began: "Wave of Illness in Woods Village" and went on to describe in small capitals that eighty men on the Emporium Forestry Company's payroll were stricken, and that there were "Hardly Enough

Well to Care for Sick." The contagion was not typhoid this time, but influenza. The article stated:

> "With one death and many in a critical condition from influenza and pneumonia, the wave of illness that has spread over this section during the past ten days is most serious. Dr. Paul H. Lowrey and three nurses are working day and night to combat the disease. . . . Eighty men on the Emporium Forestry Company's pay-roll are ill. These men are divided between the mill here and the various lumber camps operated by the company in the vicinity of Cranberry Lake and Conifer. . . . Fred Aldrich, aged about 60 years, . . . and recently a lumberjack employed by the company, died last week. His body was unclaimed and buried by the town at Benson Mines. Aldrich was a pneumonia victim. . . . There are hardly enough well to aid the doctor and nurses in the care of the sick. Several cases are reported critical."[20]

The article got the attention of Dr. Lowrey, the company physician who had succeeded Dr. Cohen. Concerned about these press reports, he also sensed a public relations disaster in the making and acted quickly to set the record straight. On March 10, he dashed off a longhand letter to *The Tupper Lake Herald* complaining of its "grossly exaggerated" description of the "dimensions and severity of the epidemic of influenza which we have had at Conifer and Cranberry Lake." Lowrey admitted there had been a lot of flu in the villages, however, he pointed out that while it was high in morbidity (number of cases), it was "extremely low in its mortality." After all, the doctor cautioned, one death out of one hundred cases really was not very serious. Besides the company's operations "are running night and day and have been since January 1. The Emporium are [sic] doing more business than was done by them a year or even two or three years ago. We feel that our sickness here has been a part of the great epidemic raging statewide and that it is has been no more severe than in other localities." Asking that the editor reverse and correct "the pernicious ill-advised" article, Lowrey finally got to the heart of the problem. It was not so much that there was an epidemic, but rather that "commercial travelers tell us that they had been told to avoid Conifer and Cranberry Lake because of this epidemic." The economic motive had apparently shoved aside the physician's humanitarian concerns. He closed by stressing that "such a slogan is not only untrue but disastrous to the welfare of both communities."

On March 15, Clyde Sykes wrote similar letters to the *Watertown*

Daily Times, The Post Standard and another to *The Tupper Lake Herald.*
The businessman's concern about a public image of a sickly and disease-
ridden place was evident. He wrote:

> "Our attention has been called to certain articles appearing in a
> recent issue of your paper, referring to a very serious epidemic situa-
> tion here and at Cranberry Lake. The facts have been greatly over-
> stated, and the report which has gotten out is injuring our work. We
> have been given to understand that traveling men are afraid to come
> here and that workmen seeking employment are avoiding us because
> of these articles. . . . The facts are that we have had a number of cases
> of influenza and grippe as has prevailed generally throughout the
> country. These cases generally were not severe and but one death re-
> sulted at Cranberry Lake. While our physician has had a busy time, he
> has not been overworked to the breaking point nor has he required the
> assistance of three trained nurses. . . . At a recent meeting of the official
> board of the Conifer Church the pastor reported that during a period
> of two and one-half years as pastor, he had not had a single funeral."[21]

Harold Johnson, president and editor of the *Watertown Daily Times*
replied to Sykes that he would print his letter, but made no mention of
a retraction nor did anyone else.

By the 1950s, communicable disease and epidemics were no longer a
major problem among loggers. The accident rate, however, continued
and was higher than in any other nationwide industry. A high percent-
age of accidents still occurred from the use of very sharp tools, heavy
lifting and frequently falling objects. With a general lack of training programs and inadequate training among local woods workers, the severity
of injuries was also more acute in the forest than elsewhere. In Hamilton
County in the 1950s, felling and bucking accounted for 56% of all disabling injuries among loggers; skidding for 21%; loading for 18%. The
most frequently damaged parts of a logger's anatomy were, not surprisingly, the lower extremities for a total of 48%; while injuries to the
trunk accounted for 25%; 11% to the arms and hands. The Hamilton
County percentages approximated those for the nation as a whole.[22]

In the 1960s and 1970s, safety became an increasingly popular subject in the pages of trade journals such as *The Lumber Camp News* and in
government publications, both state and national. Editors used comic
strip cartoon humor to portray what carelessness and ignorance could
cost an individual in the woods. But had there been much progress? On
February 1, 1987, *The New York Times* reported that "under the best

conditions, logging is a hazardous way to make a living." Whether with
axe or chainsaw, horse or tractor, river drive or truck, getting logs down
and out to market was as risky in the 1980s as it was in the 1880s. The
risk of injury on the job is still so great that carriers who provide insurance coverage for woods workers are pricing many small operators
(who typify the modern Adirondack logging industry) out of existence.

From ancient practice to high-tech mechanization, much of the character of early logging has changed. But the accident rate has remained
fairly constant. Horace Greeley's *Great Industries of the United States*
informed readers, in 1872, that for "hardy loggers, no time of their stay
in the woods is exempt from peril. Wounds are accidentally received
from the axe; limbs torn from falling trees, and branches broken by
them from other trees, made brittle by intense frost, flying in all direc-
tions threaten injury and endanger life. Their career is all hardship and
danger while their occupation is of immense importance. . . ."[23]

It is a commentary on our times that, after more than one hundred
years the threat remains the same, only the costs have gone up, both in
human and monetary terms. Whether to conserve men or trees seems a
simple choice. But in the history of the logging industry in New York
State, particularly in the North Country, trees often came before the
welfare of the woods workers.

CHAPTER SIX

The Woods Ablaze

"The women fought two nights, all night
long. . . . I say they fought fire better than the
men . . . and were more thorough in putting
it out than the men."
        —*A. W. Skiff*, Onchiota, 1903

While accidents and epidemics threatened the ability to harvest the raw material—trees—the possibility of devastation of the raw material itself presented other problems. Logging was a business intended to make money. Fires, particularly those carelessly started were an anathema to both the lumberman and the concerned citizen (the conservationist). To the former, it meant loss of revenue; to the latter, it meant what he feared the most—the wilderness laid waste by man's own hand. By the 1880s, New York State had taken a leading role in the prevention of forest fires consonant with the support it had given the preservation of the Adirondacks in general.

With the creation of the Forest Preserve in May 1885, the Empire State had been the first in the nation to formulate and enact legislation aimed at the prevention of forest fires. The protective legislation mandated that "The lands now or hereafter constituting the forest preserve shall be forever kept as wild forest lands." It also established a three-member Forest Commission to manage the Preserve. In 1892, the New

York state legislature further protected the Adirondacks by establishing the Adirondack Park within which the state-owned Forest Preserve and privately-held land co-existed. In 1895, the "forever wild" protection of Forest Preserve land became part of the New York State Constitution. As Article VII states, it clearly prohibits the cutting of timber on, as well as the selling and leasing of, state land.

By the 1890s, in the opinion of many persons, the population had been well educated in the handling of fire in the woods. "Carefulness," reported the state Forest Commission, "has taken the place of carelessness." The Forest Commission, by 1895, had its regulations posted everywhere: "Their rules are printed plainly on large placards which are posted conspicuously in hotels, stores, post-offices, schoolhouses and sawmills." For outdoors, the rules were "printed on white muslin posters, which are nailed on barns, fences, and trees along the trails and 'carrys' leading through the forest." Throughout the Adirondacks and the Catskills, "over 10,000 copies of these rules are kept posted all the time." New York's State Forestry Law required:

> " . . . the firewarden of every town in which a forest fire of more than one acre in extent has occurred within a year shall report to the Forest Commission the extent of area burned over, to the best of his information, together with the probable amount of property destroyed specifying the value of timber, as near as may be, and amount of cordwood, logs, bark or other forest product, and of fences, bridges and buildings that have been burned."[1]

These reports were condensed and published in the "Annual Reports" of the Forest, Fish and Game Commission.

In 1900, 1909, 1910 and 1916, the state passed progressively stiffer laws governing the control of forest fires. For example, the 1900 law, after some bad fires in 1899, required the appointment of "Fire wardens in every town having lands which were part of the Forest Preserve." These became known as the fire towns. In addition, railroad companies had to clean all inflammable material from their right-of-ways twice a year and "employ a patrol, and provide spark arresters on locomotives." In 1909, a penalty was enacted that assessed one year in prison and a fine of $250 for negligence causing a fire on forest lands of the state; a year later, the legislature increased the fine to $2,000 and imprisonment and made it a felony.

These enactments were followed in May 1916, by what is referred to as the General Forestry Act or the Conservation Law. It revised and spelled out even more clearly the earlier legislation governing fire control in the towns of the forest preserve. According to Professor A. B. Recknagel of Cornell University,

> "The new law provided that in fire towns, which were comprised within the forest preserve areas and were specially named in the Act, the Forest Commission must maintain a force of forest rangers, observers, and fire wardens, and the equipment necessary to prevent and extinguish forest fires. . . . Every state official having a duty to fight forest fires might temporarily employ men at fifteen cents per hour and foremen at twenty-five cents per hour for fire fighting and might summon any male person of eighteen years or over to assist in fire control."

It was advantageous to keep the wages paid recruited fire-fighters to a minimum for fear of someone deliberately making work. The act also gave the governor authority to prohibit camping, hunting, fishing and trapping when dangerous fire conditions prevailed that were contrary to the public interest. Federal law, by 1911, had authorized the Secretary of Agriculture to cooperate with any state or groups of states in maintaining "a system of fire protection on any private or State forest lands." By 1921, the federal government was allotting $25,000 to New York for cooperative fire protection; that year, with added state contributions, the total for fire protection equalled $190,443. Recknagel pointed out a year later that "New York spends more on fire protection that any other state in the Union."[2]

Strengthened legislation and ensuing laws were prompted in part by serious fires which aroused public opinion and preceded public action. The year 1903 was particularly bad. There had been no rain in the mountains other than local showers between the first week in April and the second week of June. May had been by most accounts the driest month since 1826. In the spring of 1903 Saranac Lake saw two separate instances when the temperature was over eighty; on May 27, it was eighty-five degrees with wind out of the south; and on the sixth and seventh of June the thermometer read ninety degrees in the shade. Signs and portents were not good. With alarming frequency, fires appeared in April along the right-of-ways of the New York Central, the New York and Ottawa, the Chateaugay and the Saranac and Lake Placid railroads. Fires followed in the wake of every train that passed by. One example:

> "The New York Central, from Fulton Chain to Mountain View, was bordered with smoke and flames, except on the eight-mile stretch

through the private preserve of Dr. W. Seward Webb, where a large number of patrols were employed at his expense to follow each train, night or day, and extinguish the locomotive sparks that fell along the road."[3]

High winds and extreme dryness spread spark fires very quickly and the capriciousness of the wind increased the danger of being cut off and surrounded. In Township 41, in the southwestern Adirondacks, fire burning in the big timber along an inlet of Big Moose Lake caused the water to become so hot that the pool's surface was thickly covered with dead fish, mostly trout. The railroads were asked to check the condition of all spark arresters on their locomotives; carelessness, however, allowed many to go out uninspected, so they continued to be a source of trouble along the right-of-ways where sparks ignited the bone-dry brush and undergrowth.

In the Adirondacks that summer, the resident population was not large enough to deploy around-the-clock patrols along the rail lines; New York Central was called upon to help out, and "sent several carloads of Italian laborers to assist in the work along their line" at its own expense. This was followed quickly by a decision of the Adirondack Division superintendent to send enough help so that a man could be stationed every mile along the Saranac branch. Freight trains were split in two hoping to reduce needed engine power and hence decrease spark-laden exhaust; even daily schedules were cut. Not all railroad companies complied with pleas for help; the Saranac and Lake Placid line exhibited indifference. The fires it started burned menacingly close to the villages' hotels. Interestingly, on the nineteen miles of track which constituted the Raquette Lake Railway running through state forest land from Clearwater to Durant "no fires occurred, because in granting a charter for this road the Legislature stipulated that the locomotives must use petroleum for fuel." By and large, the railroads and their owners were anxious that their locomotives be held blameless as to the cause of fires, since the companies themselves were legally responsible for the damage caused by their carriers. The railroads, in fact, took considerable interest in preserving the north woods as their summer tourist traffic depended upon it.

Trains, in 1903, were not the only source of trouble since not all the fires in the North Country that year started along the tracks. It seemed that unsportsmanlike conduct might also be blamed.

"At this season of the year there are a large number of fishermen in the woods, many of them belonging to a careless, shiftless class, unworthy of the name of sportsmen. They employ no guides, but straggle aimlessly through the forests, camping out wherever night overtakes them. As they move on from place to place they generally leave their camp fires burning; when they make coffee at noon they make little or no effort to extinguish the small fire kindled for that purpose. With the woods as dry as they were last spring, several fires, which started up in remote, unfrequented places, were fairly attributable to fishermen of this class, some of whom were reported as having been seen in these localities."[4]

Prosecuting offenders was difficult—evidence was hard to come by and local juries sympathized with defendants, often refusing to render guilty verdicts.

There were other reasons for the 1903 fires. Among them were the "incendiaries and degenerates prompted by malice, revenge, or criminal instincts"; those "set by men in order to get employment"; and still others caused by "the ever increasing number of residents." Lastly there were "the farmers who are carrying on agricultural operations of a minor character, and by the large number of men who remain in the region after the lumbering operations on which they were employed have ceased. Fifty years ago, when there were scarcely any people in our woods, forest fires were almost unknown." Perhaps worst of all was the "laxity of public opinion which prevails in certain parts of the Adirondack region." Nearly every village has

" . . . a disreputable class whose presence is inimical to the preservation of our forests. They are the men who, having been arrested at some time for violation of the Game Law or timber stealing, have grievance against the authorities. They hang around hotels or taverns and when any so-called 'State man' is in hearing, delight in making threats that, 'The State has got to look out or there will be more fires in the woods,' to which the bystanders listen with smiles or nods of approval."[5]

Citing the reasons for the cause of fires did not put them out. William Fox, the superintendent of state forests, reported:

"As the fires increased in number it became difficult to get men enough to fight them. . . . A great many who turned out willingly and fought fire at the start abandoned the work after a while, explaining that they could not afford to labor any longer and wait on the town nine months for their pay. I then made an arrangement with some of the lumber companies, whose lands were in danger, to send in all the men they could spare from their jobs and to advance the cash needed to pay them promptly, the companies to wait for reimbursement until the towns could settle the account. Under this agreement a large number of experienced woodsmen were set to work."[6]

Fox was faced with a virtually impossible task. He confided in his report that

" . . . under the weather conditions no earthly power or organization could prevent this evil when locomotives were daily kindling fires in dry grass . . . , and wandering fishermen were leaving their smudge and coffee fires burning in the woods uncared for. . . . Where a fire occurred at any considerable distance from a camp or boarding-house, the crew was ordered to remain there all night and sleep on the ground, arrangements having been made at the same time to send in food and blankets to them. This involved no hardship, as the men were used to camping out; moreover, the nights, with one exception, were warm, and there was no rain. In each case of this kind the fire-warden was ordered to make a contract for food supplies and some simple camp equipment at the nearest store, lumber camp, hotel or boarding-house, and to detail one or more men with pack-baskets to carry in this material."

Fox gave the forest commissioners to understand that the task was not an easy one and that, in fact,

" . . . 6,487 men were ordered out by the wardens, and that the total number of [man-] days worked at the fires in the Adirondacks amounted to 77,290. Moreover, there was only a sparse population to draw from. Hamilton County, one of the largest in the State, has only 4,947 people all told—men, women and children. Had it not been for the active, efficient work of the wardens and their men during this prolonged drought, the numerous fires would have coalesced— 'run together,' as it is termed—and the Adirondack forest would have been destroyed, leaving nothing but a bare and blackened ruin throughout its entire extent."[7]

What was the cost of the horrible spring and summer fires of 1903? Fox, from all reports submitted to him, estimated the following:

Acres of timber land burned..292,121
Acres of brush land burned...172,068
Value of standing timber destroyed...$666,207
Value of logs, pulp-wood, etc. destroyed.................................$145,457

Value of buildings burned...$34,418
Total number of days' labor...77,290
Acres of State timber land burned...33,698
Acres of State brush land burned...24,420

Elaborating on the statistics, Fox gave a sobering impression of the destructiveness of fire in the forest.

> "The percentage of virgin forest was small. By far the greater part of the timber burned was on what are known as lumbered lands, such as the State had been buying for one dollar and fifty cents per acre, but which, through the recent rise in value for this class of property, are now worth from two dollars to three dollars per acre. Some lands of this class, situated near a railroad, or otherwise accessible, are worth more. . . . The loss in buildings, fences, etc., includes the large hotel south of North Elba, known as the Adirondack Lodge; the Loomis Camp, on Little Tupper Lake; several miles of wire fence on Nehasane Park, and several barns or outbuildings at various places. The loss in logs, pulp-wood, etc., includes the large amount of acid wood that was cut and piled on the lands of the Brooklyn Cooperage Company; several thousand cords of pulp-wood and cordwood, belonging to the Chateaugay Iron and Ore Company, piled at Plumadore Station, Franklin County; numerous skidways of logs left in the woods last winter through lack of snow, and piles of cordwood in forests near villages or shipping points."[8]

The causes of the great fire of 1903 were catalogued and quantified by Fox as follows:

Railroad locomotives	121	Wintergreen pickers	3
Burning fallows	88	Lunatic	1
From other fires by wind	61	Dooryard fire	1
Fishermen	47	Children at play	1
Tobacco smokers	23	Smoking out a hedgehog	1
Hunters	7	Burning a straw bed	1
Incendiaries	6	Burning brakes (ferns)	1
Camp fires	6	Blasting stone	1
Burning buildings	6	Sparks from torch	1
Sparks from chimneys	3	Lightning	1

Eighteen years later, in 1921, when fire damage was the worst experienced since 1903, the causes had changed a bit. Laws had become more stringent; locomotives had been made safer and less damaging to the forest; tourism had increased and with it the likelihood of fire; and, finally, smoking had become more widespread, particularly the use of cigarettes.⁹ A table for the three years 1919-1921 lists smokers as the greatest culprits but, of course, the cyclical vagaries of weather and the watchfulness of the population must be factored into all generalizations involving the causes of forest fires.¹⁰

What do fires mean to those who have experienced them? The homesteader on the blazing prairie and the forest dweller with the woods ablaze experience equally the reality of a holocaust or inferno. For fire wardens and others living in the mountains, the fiery year of 1903 was unforgettable. Personal accounts exist from nearly every corner of the Adirondacks, and convey the sense of danger—the concern for loss of life and property—that has a realistic ring today for anyone who lives surrounded by miles and miles of trees.

"We had a drought lasting sixty days," wrote George Meader from Dannemora in Clinton County. He had "worked two days in putting out fire at the edge of a 600-acre tract of State land" near the prison. From Ausable Forks, William Hopkins observed "for seven weeks not one drop of rain fell." He did not think any of the fires "were of incendiary origin." At Ausable Chasm, Charles Giddings fought "a very hot fire; the young timber was mostly killed. . . . We fought it for three days against a strong south wind" before the wind shifted to the west and the fire was put out. At Newman, in Essex County, B. R. Brewster's "fire was worst of all." On June 3, "a terrible wind arose" about noon and "carried the sparks through the woods at a terrible rate." Near the "South Meadows and Adirondack Lodge about 6,000 acres had been lumbered. The Spruce and Balsam brush made good fuel." In the course of the afternoon, "the fire swept over an area of 10,000 acres." In Olmstedville, someone complained of the slash left by last year's logging which had taken "all the large timber . . . but now everything is killed."¹¹

In the east, at Chesterfield, fire warden C. W. Rowe indicted the railroad for the summer's trouble. According to Rowe,

> "The Delaware and Hudson Railroad has about ten miles of track in this town—nearly all of it along a mountain side, and with very few buildings in sight of the road. This mountain side was covered with forest when the railroad was built, but it has been burned over so many times since that nearly all the timber has been killed and is falling down, making excellent fuel for a forest fire. . . . The fires in this town are now under control, but the engines on the Delaware and Hudson Railroad set fires on the mountain south of Port Kent nearly every day. . . . Their fire screens are not worth a straw. . . . I venture

After a fire at Kildare in 1912.

Lumbering slash from tree-topping and de-limbing littered thousands of acres providing readily combustible material.

Spark arresters became mandatory for all locomotives operating in the North Woods but were frequently inadequate. Spark arrester on Grasse River Railroad locomotive.

Railroad companies sensitive to negative public relations began to make greater efforts to protect the woods from fires started by their locomotives. New York Central Fire Service train.

Wealthy landowners like the Webbs, Whitneys and the Durants maintained their own fire vigils along the right-of-ways. Ne-Ha-Sa-Ne Park Fire Service.

In 1912 the Bell Telephone Company built a telephone line from Childwold to the top of Mt. Arab, not far from Conifer. The Sykes contributed a fire tower which commanded a view of most of their holdings.

to say that 100 fires have been set by engines on this road within sight of my residence, a distance of four or five miles."[12]

At Westport on Lake Champlain, Charles Hooper "spoke to the station agent . . . about the railroad fires and he got quite mad about it." The agent said, "the railroad was blamed for everything," but admitted there was little that could be done about the escaping sparks. Besides, "most of the damage is done by freight trains." At Elizabethtown, an estimate of buildings destroyed included: "Euba Mills, $2,000; house, barn and blacksmith shop, $1,000; three tenant houses ($500 each), $1,500; one farmhouse, barn and out buildings, $1,500; total, $6,000." Evidently though, "no fences or bridges of any value were destroyed."

From Ellenburg in Franklin County, George McKinney complained of high winds and the spruce tops which had been left on the ground through which the fire ran at a fast clip. At Reynoldston on June 9, the fire "came from the adjoining town of Dickinson, and could be controlled only on the virgin forest land" where it was checked "by continual work until rain came." Fremont Smith from Loon Lake condemned "the donkey engines" which were being used on the road building job: "We cannot keep men enough over there to keep the fire out, as they start flames wherever they go. I don't think they are using any screens at all." The most disheartening report was from Perkins Smith of St. Regis Falls who "went over the burned acres (300 acres) and found that it was entirely virgin forest, heavily timbered with White Pine." He thought the pine would "not die for two or three years yet, . . . but a large amount of pulp timber was standing which was badly damaged." At Onchiota manpower was spread so thin that A. N. Skiff

> " . . . got the women out to help. If I hadn't done so nothing could have stopped the fire from burning every building for miles around here. The women fought two nights, all night long, waded brooks clear to their knees. I say they fought fire better than the men, they were that scared, and were more thorough in putting it out. . . . "

Skiff felt women fire-fighters ought to be paid the same as the men.

> "Up in the town of Brighton they had women fighting fire and they got their pay the same as the men. There are lots of times when the fires are raging so bad that everyone has to turn out. I am going to send this account to you and see if you don't think they ought to have their pay. I say it is a shame if they don't, and I think you will say the same."[13]

The women, in fact, got paid.

Hamilton County had its problems, too. At Indian Lake, fire got out of hand and ran in high wind. By May 2, it was nearly out and damage was reported as little. At Inlet, Wellington Kenwell had all his men out carrying water, some through the night. They had

" . . . the fire all out by morning. The three men connected a pipe line, turning a one and one half inch stream of water on the burning ground. We kept this pipe line running for three weeks. One fire started opposite the mouth of Indian River, just above the Beecher Camp. I think it was started by a smoker, as there were parties fishing there. The fire on Lime Kiln Lake was started by parties camping there. I employed a man to get the names of the sportsmen who were seen there the day before the fire was discovered. This case seems easy of proof. Smokers start most of the fires in this locality. A match thrown down, or a pipe knocked out, will start a fire in a few minutes."

At Long Lake, W. D. Jennings had to send to Newcomb for help "and by June first we had 125 men on the line back-firing and trenching."[14]

The sweep of the terrain involved in 1903 and the logistics available to cope would give anyone pause. At Wells, east of Speculator, there were three fires going on in the town. Frank Stanyon wrote seriously that "it is the opinion of our citizens that these fires are started to make feed for deer." At Nehasane, Byron Ames simply described the situation as "trying and desperate, . . . the wonder is that the destruction was not greater." J. E. Roberts had a busy time at Old Forge, if for no other reason than the difficulty in getting accurate reports from the field. Many were exaggerated. For example,

" . . . the fire at Fulton Chain is not the same as when you were here. Another one caught near the railroad and is burning on the east side of the track below Fulton Chain, but I have it under control. I have sixty men at the Big Moose fire, and have notified the warden in Long Lake, as it is outside of this town by three miles. The fire at Beaver River is burning slowly, but Bullock is doing good work and keeping it from spreading. It is so far through the woods to the fire on Watson's East Triangle that I have asked Miller to take care of it from the town of Croghan. A new fire started on the land of the Adirondack League Club, caused by a campfire. It burned fiercely, but tonight I have it down in good shape. . . . Many of the fires are greatly exaggerated by people who tell what they hear but don't go near the fires at all."[15]

Up at Big Moose, the firefighters were getting tired. "Sixty men [were] on the ground day and night . . . in heat and smoke." J. H. Higby, hard-pressed, wanted to know, "how many hours is a day's work? The men say eight hours." No matter what anyone thought, Higby was "keeping the time by the hour." At the same time in Harrisville, Lewis County, "the air is so full of smoke that we could not see a fresh fire when it started. The whole country seemed to be on fire at once." To the north, in St. Lawrence County, J. F. Evans of Fine felt

> " . . . the past week has been the worst time for fires that I have seen in years. The entire woods in the west half of this town, and, in fact, clear to Cranberry Lake, are on fire. The New York Central Railroad started seven fires on one run last week from Carthage to Oswegatchie. This fire is burning from the line of the railroad and Bear Lake clear through the woods. I have had out nearly seventy men at times."[16]

In Hopkinton, Arthur Flanders "came out of the woods on Friday night (May thirtieth) for the first time to get a day off since May eighth. . . . There are about 4,000 acres burned over, mostly lumbered land."

Newspapers carried accounts that reinforced those of the wardens. *The Evening Journal* at Glens Falls reported on June 9, 1903: "Yesterday, at Indian Lake, some cattle were turned out in a swamp which had been burned over but which was apparently free from fire by reason of the recent rains. However, the cattle sank into the soft earth and fire burst forth in several places, seriously burning the animals." *The Troy Record* five days earlier informed its readers that "at Twin Pond, on the Chateaugay Railroad, a wooden trestle took fire from the forest fires, and a freight engine broke through, carrying Engineer Kelly down with it. He escaped . . . with slight bruises." What happened to the engine was not reported. Lastly, there was the harrowing tale of George McDonald's camps close to Tupper Lake which were reported destroyed by the *Essex County Republican* on May 29, 1903. The story stated that

> " . . . Mrs. Joseph Prevost had given birth to a child only a few hours before. She was carried on a mattress to the railway, where she was placed on a hand-car and removed from danger. Members of her rescuing party were severely burned. . . . A woman was left in one of the camps through some mistake, and when this was discovered George McDonald and Chester Carr ran through the flames and rescued her. They found her on her knees praying, and, strange to say, this camp did not burn, although another, a short distance away seemingly in

much less danger, was destroyed."[17]

Amazingly, the great fire of 1903 seemingly spared most men and women of the North Country; although there were reports of loss of life, most were unverified. For example, two railhands of the New York Central got separated from their work gang, wandered into the woods and were presumed lost and burned. This was never substantiated. As William Fox points out, "in view of the thousands of men who were at work under extremely dangerous conditions it is a matter of congratulation that there was no greater loss of life."

What did fire mean to the large private, logging companies? First of all, burning trees meant burning dollars; no businessman wanted to see his raw material and processing mills go up in smoke. Carefulness was preached since precautions against fire in the woods translated into protection of profits. Still, when fire safety became institutionalized the presence of foresters, fire wardens, and government—both people and paper—at times seemed an undue encroachment of free enterprise and the rights of property owners. Many persons in the Adirondacks in the early twentieth century were (and still are) affronted when it appeared that controls, either state or federal, were limiting their freedom of action. Nevertheless, when the campaign for preventing forest fires began and controls were tightened, the loggers went along. Indeed, many lumbermen gave lip-service to and practiced aspects of scientific forest management. It was simply in their own best interest to do so even if they were not necessarily converted to the cause. Meanwhile, they had an eye cast over their shoulder to see what new rules and regulations might be enacted which would increase their operational costs.

The large logging companies did not want fires; but neither did they want or welcome scrutiny by a host of government men roaming the woods looking for code violations. The prevailing attitude was amusingly revealed by Clyde Sykes in 1912 when he hastily wrote his colleagues: "Mr. Hayes the patrolman will be at Conifer Monday A.M. to give you a fire permit." Not very alarming nor revealing until the men were instructed: "Do not have any fires going when he comes. He acted as if he knew we had been breaking the law and burning without permits." This approach to compliance was not peculiar to the Emporium Forestry Company nor to Adirondack logging in general. It was simply a mind-set of persons who acted first and applied for permits later, believing, since time was money, they would not waste it. They preferred to pay a fine rather than miss an important shipment or delay a customer's order.

The Emporium Forestry Company held well over 120,000 acres of Adirondack timberland and the company's concern for fire prevention was typical of that voiced by other large Adirondack operators in the first decades of the twentieth century. The scars of the great fires which had burned in and around Cranberry Lake were still very apparent when W. L. Sykes and his sons began business in the Adirondacks in 1912. Their logging operations were inseparably related to the Grasse River Railroad and to the many tram roads which they built into the woods to move the cutting crews in and the hardwood out. The careful maintenance of railroad right-of-ways and logging roads was prescribed by New York law. The term "logging road" was to be construed to mean any railroad branch, line or division, or independent line, the chief or main business of which is the transportation of logs, lumber or other forest products. Regulations and specifications were outlined by the state Conservation Commission. They were sent to railroad operators, and specified the tolerances required for spark arresters and ash pans. They were very precise. Arresting screens were to be made of "wire netting or its equivalent with opening not exceeding the opening in wire netting 2½ x 2½ meshes per inch with wire not less than #10 B.W.G. for this mesh. No opening will be permitted at any point inside of extension front which is larger in area than ¼ x ¼ inch." Ash pan specifications were particular: "On the wide firebox engines where openings exist between the foundation ring and the top of the ash pan suitable guards must be placed and properly fastened." On narrow firebox ash pans it was important that "the back and front dampers . . . be provided with flanges on both sides and bottom of dampers which will project over pan at least 1¼ inch" and "on hopper ash pans particular attention must be given to having all joints properly protected and reinforced so that when the pan begins to warp there will not be any unreasonable openings." Failure to meet these specifications would result in a fine of one hundred dollars a day until violations were corrected.

In May 1912, W. L. Sykes wrote from the Ten Eyck Hotel in Albany to his partner William Caflisch at Conifer telling him that the Conservation Commission had "requested us to meet here" with them. These were "the State forest men" and W. L. was anxious to "try to get our matters so adjusted so as to get along well with them." In the meantime, Sykes suggested, "I hope you will be able to get a good wire spark arrester on the log loader and Eng. 42 so it will show on the top of the stack that it is safe." At the beginning of 1912, as the company was gearing up its operations, there was more cutting, millwork, and railroad construction which increased the possibility of fire. On January 13, it received a letter from William O'Brien at Fulton Chain, superintendent of fire district number three, stating that "the Conservation Commission has built a telephone line from Childwold Station to the top of Arab Mountain [outside Conifer], the same to connect with the Bell Telephone Co. for the purpose of locating forest fires." O'Brien went on to say that

" . . . a tower will have to be built, I have been informed that your Co. have [sic] a wind mill tower, not in use at Cranberry Lake. The Commission advises me that they would like to purchase, and will pay $15.00 for this tower, this observation station will cover a large portion of your lands in locating Forest Fires not covered by any other Mt. Station, as a tower will have to be built on this mountain in readiness for the Fire Season."[18]

The state was taking considerable interest in the new company operating at Conifer.

The company's own assessment of its fire readiness was high. "We are fairly well protected from fire," wrote Sykes in November, 1912, "there are three state observation stations overlooking our land, and we have some methods of our own, such as fire extinguishers on our locomotives." After conferring with C. R. Pettis, the state Superintendent of Forests, the following memorandum of record was drawn and signed by both W. L. Sykes and the superintendent. It was mutually agreed at this meeting to discuss "the question of patrol on tramroads, in order to obtain adequate forest fire protection." Further

" . . . the Company suggests at least a one-man patrol on foot or with a speeder to cover all tramroads operated by the Company, the general plan being that the patrolman would follow each train at a suitable distance. It is also understood that there will be installed and maintained telephone lines, water barrels, time clocks, or other arrangements of this kind, as mutually agreed upon. . . ."[19]

"As to the fire record," Clyde Sykes wrote in 1931, "since 1912 we have had a planing mill burn in 1920. This is the only fire of any size aside from some dwelling houses the Company has ever had." Unfortunately the planing mill fire was serious. On February 5, 1920, Clyde Sykes wrote to Emporium's Utica office "in order that you may be informed as to the fire which destroyed our Conifer planing mill. . . ." The fire was reported about 12:20 a.m. and was put out by 5:00 p.m. The cause was unknown. However,

> " . . . the planing mill building proper was entirely destroyed from the packing floor up and the working floor itself has fallen through the basement over a good part of the building. The old log camps on the Northern side of the building were saved as was also the dock leading to the planing mill and the storage shed West of the planing mill. The planing mill was operating on a day and night shift and several of the night crew who did not go to their homes for their midnight lunch were in the building when it took fire. . . . The pumps and fire fighting apparatus worked very well and for a time it seemed as though the fire had been checked with perhaps but slight damage to the building. It kept breaking out . . . afresh until the entire building was destroyed."

The loss was a heavy one but Sykes was optimistic that not all "of the machinery that was in the planing mill building proper is a complete loss. . . ."[20]

A major fire and a typhoid epidemic made 1920 a bad year for Emporium. The company not only became very aware of its public health posture but also quickly showed renewed interest in fire protection. In July 1920, Professor Recknagel of Cornell wrote the Sykes that because of "the increased cutting of hardwoods in the Adirondacks," the disposal of hardwood brush was getting to be a problem. He wished to gather field information similar to that which had been gathered prior to the introduction of the "Lopping Law," so important to the reduction and control of fires. Recknagel wanted one of his graduate students in forestry to do the study at Conifer. Sykes, a bit gun-shy, wrote back that he would be pleased to cooperate but reminded Recknagel that in

> "some instances where photography is used pictures have been used which have worked to the detriment of people in the lumber business. While a note of warning may be unnecessary we want to be guarded so that in studying the Hardwood slashing you do not work a hardship rather than a benefit."[21]

In other words, do not get carried away and end up getting legislation passed and laws enacted that are going to cost us a lot of money in the long run.

In December 1920, W. L. Sykes was still involved with the insurance claims and the rebuilding of the planing mill. He was in a very fire-conscious frame of mind. Two days before Christmas, he wrote to the woods superintendent at Conifer and to his assistant at Cranberry Lake: "Now that men are plentier . . . we will be enabled to give more attention to the cleaning up of the right-of-ways of the tram roads and along the right-of-way of the Grasse River." Sykes told them "to clean up as much as possible the combustible material" so when the fire season comes we "will be better prepared to prevent fires starting . . . in our timber lands." Drawing on his long experience, Sykes told them

> "I wish especially to call attention to the importance of encouraging the growth of Hemlock, Pine, Balsam, Tamarack and Spruce on and along the right-of-ways of the tram roads so as to keep the evergreen and the Tamarack growing as thick as possible as a protection from fire because they will hold the moisture and prevent the growth of weeds and brush."[22]

Not only was Sykes a knowledgeable woodsman, he was also a shrewd businessman, well aware of the importance of image. "Trees," he wrote, "which are dead or dying or blown down along the tramroads should be gathered up as fast as possible and brought to the mills." This also had to be done along the main line of the Grasse River. He wanted "at least one man that will use good judgment so as to not injure the telephone lines by falling trees across them or in anyway injuring other trees." This was the woodsman talking. The businessman and politician then took over. "You know," he confided to his boys, "the opinion of the general public is often formed by the appearance of the right-of-way of the railroad and also the officers of the Commissions."

When it came to protecting their interests from fire, the Sykes did a good job; but they always, or almost always, claimed that the state commissions required it. Perhaps this was a subconscious resentment of state control and oversight. In a 1922 letter to Ellwood Wilson, manager of the Laurentide Company of Grand Mére, Quebec, W. L. Sykes stated the case directly:

> "We are operating here under what may be termed the most diffi-cult of any lumber operation in the country because of the fact of being within the State Forest Preserve some very hard and difficult rules are in practice as a matter of preserving the forest from fire, all of which adds to the expense, but in the long run may prove money well spent."[23]

In addition, Sykes was sure that he could also show Wilson some of the best safety devices "on our locomotives that are used anywhere." In the short term, too much state oversight was a burden—but Sykes was not a fool. Although controls cost money, he took pride in the adaptations made to the company's locomotives and in his awareness that fire was the logger's greatest enemy. Clyde Sykes, writing a former Syracuse University friend, told him that in the business at Conifer

> " . . . we use approximately 3,000 to 3,500 tons of soft coal annually and in the summer time require a very lumpy coal on account of the fact that the State Commissions require us to screen the front ends of our locomotives with a very fine screen to prevent the escape of sparks and remove the hazard of possible forest fires from locomotives."[24]

The senior Sykes' views on government regulation in general and fire in particular were probably best stated in Utica in November 1914. He was at the ninth annual meeting of the Empire State Forest Products Association and in his report as chairman of the forestry committee, he stressed that "fire protection cannot be emphasized too strongly . . . wherever there are forests, young or mature." But, he added, "I believe there has been too much persecution of the railroads. . . . I think the railroads have been made to suffer altogether too much," particularly from unreasonable laws such as removing "all grass, brush or other inflammable materials" with the unreasonable emphasis on "ALL." It was a tragedy, Sykes felt, that many laws passed to regulate various activities were passed by men "who are absolutely ignorant of the conditions that the laws are to regulate." He thought that much of the regulatory legislation was "misguided" and "vicious." What was the solution to be? Public education was the answer, i.e., lobbying. If the people knew the facts, things might get better. "We are," complained Sykes, "ruled by commission after commission, and it is hoped that some of the commissions will be done away with after awhile, so that there will be a chance to breathe." Railroads were all too often indicted as the cause of Adirondack forest fires. The populist sentiments of the day simply added more heat to the condemnation of railroads in general.

Still, those persons who owned railroads that ran through their own forested lands admitted a "desire to protect the property from fires, and they are ready and willing to do anything within reason to accomplish this object." In the Adirondacks, whether it was the fire laws, the top-lopping laws or the workmen's compensation law, "the question is everlastingly coming up of the rights of the owners against the rights of the public." For the most part the majority of the logging fraternity agreed that the forest ablaze was a worse alternative than government regulation. The final act in this saga of North Country logging was the slow but sure move to conservative practices by the Emporium Forestry Company and its competitors. It is, in essence, the evolution of a company policy toward what was to become acceptable logging methods in the Adirondacks.

CHAPTER SEVEN

Conservative Forestry: An Epilogue

"There was a noble grove of pines on the high bank of Long Lake just above the outlet. The year after the dam was built their trunks had disappeared."

—*L. E. Chittenden*, 1893

Peter Kalm, the Swedish naturalist, traveling in North America, arrived at Lake George on a cloudy day in 1749. The high mountains were obscured by the mists and rising fog, prophetically described "as the smoke of a charcoal kiln." He was told that behind the high mountains, to the west of the lake, the country was covered for miles by tall forests intersected by rivers, brooks and small lakes. Kalm's informant thought it was a region "very fit to be inhabited" and one which was covered by "vast forests of firs of the white, black, and red kind." Little more than one hundred and twenty years later, W. H. H. Murray, the Boston minister whose 1869 book *Adventures in the Wilderness; or Camp-Life in the Adirondacks* occasioned a stampede of 19th century tourists and sports to the Adirondacks, was pillorying the lumbermen as "the curse and scourge of the wilderness," who had ruined Maine but somehow had not yet destroyed "the pride and beauty" of the Adirondacks.

Murray's enthusiasm and romantic view clouded a more accurate vision of reality in the north woods. Whether Murray was aware of it or not is unknown, but by 1850 New York had already become the nation's leading lumber producer and the Adirondack forest supplied seemingly unending amounts of charcoal, lumber, tanning bark, potash and fuel wood. In Warren County, six tanneries used more than fifteen thousand cords of hemlock bark annually in 1885; earlier, the advent of a chemical process which reduced wood to pulp suitable for paper-making created a host of pulp mills. The loggers fed them soft wood until the land was mostly cleared of conifers. In addition to paper mills, there were barrel makers and the producers of wood alcohol who made other wood consumers, such as charcoal-burning iron furnaces, seem negligible by comparison. The New York State Forest Board stated that "compared with the owners of barrel and acid factories the lumbermen were harmless, for the latter seldom cut over 15 percent of the trees." At the turn of the century, with these new industries in the Adirondacks, it seemed to some that "the outlook for forest preservation is very unsat-isfactory."[1]

There was a gloomy side to Adirondack logging. By 1898, after more than thirty years of hard cutting, nearly two-thirds of the region's forests had been logged for softwoods. In retrospect, it was a litany of disaster. Virgin forest stands were completely lumbered. Timber slash littered thousands upon thousands of acres. Only the best parts of the finest trees were cut and used. Great fires ravished many sections of the mountains in 1903, 1908 and 1913. Devastation by the loggers prompted action. Between 1885, when the Forest Preserve was created, and 1894 the state experimented with statutory protection. Finally the Constitu-tional Convention of 1894 ratified what is known as the "Forever Wild" clause, Article VII, which became constitutional law in New York on January 1, 1895.

Long years of work by many individuals and groups—from colonial times forward—had finally convinced the framers of government in New York that the forests were finite. The conservationists had ac-cepted John Ruskin's credo that the earth has been lent to us by God for life, but that it must be preserved for those who come after us. Unfortu-nately, the commercial interests heard neither God nor Ruskin. They had to be convinced.

With the completion of American Independence, public-spirited citi-zens of the new republic formed voluntary associations and societies dedicated to the improvement of the useful arts. In 1791, the New York Society for the Promotion of Agriculture, Arts and Manufacturers had

Julian Rix (1850-1903) documented graphically the effects of logging on Adirondack forests. This wood engraving entitled "Destruction of Forests in the Adirondacks" was published by Harper and Brothers in 1884.

Wood engraving by Julian Rix entitled "Forest Destruction in the Adirondacks" was published in 1885 by Harper and Brothers.

Poor logging practices and an unregulated industry destroyed stream and river banks. Photograph by Seneca Ray Stoddard.

Tanneries like the Bewman Tannery near Warrensburgh consumed huge quantities of hemlock bark as tanning agent.

Courtesy of The Adirondack Museum

Charcoal burners supplied the iron furnaces with unlimited quantities of charcoal to the complete disregard of the woods. "The Path of the Charcoal Burners" *by Seneca Ray Stoddard.*

Slash covered thousands of acres in the wake of logging operations.

Pulpwood consumed unlimited quantities of spruce and pulp mills processed them with an unquenchable thirst. Thousands of logs are seen being driven on Big Tupper Lake to the mill at Piercefield.

presented to the state a plan "for increasing the growth of wood and valuable timber." The society's recommendations were not followed, but the New York State Forest Commission looked back in 1886 and acknowledged "so far as [is known], this was the first attempt made by this state in the direction of timber preservation and forest culture." Little was happening to slow the cutting of the forest. A Commission of State Parks had been authorized in 1872, and proposed to give the state title to timber lands lying within Lewis, Essex, Clinton, Franklin, St. Lawrence, Herkimer and Hamilton counties. In the interval between 1872 and 1883, when the law conveying title was finally passed, state land had continued to be sold.

The battle between the logging interests and those who feared the total destruction of the woods was fully joined. There was cultivated in the public mind a view of clear-cut and treeless mountain-scapes which threatened to end forever the ideal of sylvan grandeur, the romantic symbol of James Fenimore Cooper's Leatherstocking and the majestic vision of the Hudson River School. Conflict was inevitable. Lumber barons, on the one hand, exploited their forested kingdoms to meet the insatiable demands for wood and wood products. On the other hand, a growing urban middle class yearned to escape the oppressiveness of the city by enjoying the new-found relief of a north woods holiday. The clash between the harsh realities of the marketplace and the perpetuation of a wilderness world resolved itself only after the users, both loggers and public alike, agreed that the forest was a finite resource to be managed and harvested for the best interest of all concerned. This did not happen quickly.

Spafford's *Gazetter of the State of New York* confirmed one of the oldest facts of economic life: where raw materials and ease of transportation to market centers co-exist, there soon develops an active manufacturing interest. "Lumbering," he wrote, "is the principal object with the inhabitants and it is said that the lumber taken to Quebec this summer, 1810, by one of the inhabitants [of Massena] will amount to $60,000, the timber all taken from his own land." But there was a cost to the community because "unfortunately, agriculture is much neglected, a common case in lumbering countries." Spafford saw lumbering in 1810 as a threat to agriculture. William Fox, some eighty years later, blamed the farmer, not the loggers, for "the disappearance of the forest. . . . The farmer cuts and burns every tree and bush . . . ; the lumberman takes only a few scattered trees to the acre, confining his selection to some marketable species." Furthermore, Fox reminded his readers, fires "which destroy so much of our forest acres" were really due to farmers' carelessness and, to a lesser degree, "to locomotives, hunters, campers and several minor causes." Emphatically, Fox wrote: "The lumbermen do not start fires; for their work—chopping and log hauling—is done mostly in the late fall and winter when the woods will not take fire."[2] Fox had conveniently overlooked the slash left by the loggers as a cause of many conflagrations. The farmer was still indicted as late as 1958. Even after the Emporium Forestry Company had ceased operating, George Sykes wrote to Howard Hanlon who had recently addressed the Empire State Forest Products Association in Albany, telling him how much he liked the talk, "particularly your somewhat unique approach where you point out the clearing of farms and home sites caused the cutting of enormous forest areas before the lumbermen began operations of any size." Old ideas die slowly.

The Forest Commission warned in its first annual report in 1885, that "if the forests are destroyed, if the desolation which now everywhere marks the outer border of the forest is allowed to extend over the entire plateau, an irreplaceable asset will be the result." Five years later, in 1893, the Commission, more forcefully and succinctly than ever, reminded the legislature that "the public interests involved . . . are so vast and important that the proposed measure is entitled to your earnest consideration." Reciting the litany that had varied little over the years, the Commission contended that

> " . . . on the preservation of our forests depends the water supply of our rivers and canals; the motive power of great manufacturing interests; the priceless benefits offered by our forest sanitariums; the many delightful places of refuge from the summer heat of cities; and the existence of our fish and game. But, above all, on their preservation depends that great factor in our political economy, our future timber supply."[3]

The total area of virgin forest in the Adirondack wilderness in the 1880s was approximately twenty-five hundred square miles. The areas where the timber had never been touched by axe, fire or flood grew smaller with every passing year. Places such as Little Tupper Lake in the heart of the mountains still had "some of the most valuable timber lands" in all this region. "The woods about the lake," reported the Commission, "have never heard the lumberman's axe." In other areas, for example, on the land between the Ausable and the Saranac rivers, the forest was mowed down. Hemlock was barked for the tanneries, and everything else—the young pine, spruce, maple and birch—was simply removed *in toto* to feed the charcoal kilns. Had the Adirondacks been logged out? Not quite. But it was time for action. Much of the region was already given over to second and third growth timber.

Gilded Age entrepreneurs operated with impunity in leveling the forest and their unrestrained excesses aroused public opposition. The ruthless exploitation of the nation's natural resources—not the least among them the great forests of the country—had alarmed many persons and groups. Enlightened logging interests, state and national governments and crusaders for the cause of conservation all raised their voices in support of moderation and common sense if not for the total abolition of wasteful and destructive practices. New York's North Country provided a heated forum where opinion ranged from the most unreconstructed to the most utopian points of view. Few persons were more pessimistic about the future of the north woods than L. E. Chittenden who, writing in the 1890s, felt that the "Adirondack region is thickly sown with the germs of febrile disease." The infectious virus was the "new companies of lumbermen" who ran roughshod over the mountains, "felling every evergreen above ten inches in diameter." The loggers, thought Chittenden, may give lip service to better methods, but in the long run they would build their dams and flood more and more lowlands "in order to reach forests more remote" in the heart of the mountains. The more loggers, the more slash and debris that accumulates, and the more of both, the greater the frequency of forest fires. Every stream would have a wood-pulp mill; sanitary laws would be ignored; railroads and tourists would pollute the water and the land. "Increasing crowds of tourists, of artists, of persons who think they are sportsmen will infest the country during the summer, and the poor victims of pulmonary disease will come to it in the winter to sicken and die."

Armegeddon was at hand. For Chittenden, "the prospect of now preserving the Adirondack country . . . is very remote." The spruce, hemlock, maple and ash for construction and "the enormous consumption of wood pulp" would soon exhaust the forest. As iron furnaces expanded in such places as the small village of Clintonville, known as the great nail factory of the North Country, more and more charcoal was needed. "The trees were swept away as if some gigantic scythe-bearer had mowed [them] over . . . and where the forest had stood were huckleberry plains, where the berries were picked by Canadian-French *habitans*." It was so bad that a person could not find a tree big enough to make a decent fishing pole. Nothing, however, had done damage comparable to that done by the "army of destruction, the first invasion of the lumberman." The chance for ever greater profits spurred him on, and the results were devastating.

By 1896, the alarmist note struck by Chittenden and the forest commissioners was echoed in the popular media. *Godey's Magazine* clamored that

> " . . . the lumbermen are today clearing the north woods at the rate of 80,000 acres a year. . . . This means that, if the annual destruction goes on as usual, the woods will be wiped out in twenty years; that is, as a place of interest, of beauty, and of value. . . . Consideration not only of sentiment but of utility and public welfare demand the further protection and preservation of the Adirondack forest domain before another year rolls round."[4]

Forest and Stream in a strongly voiced protest in December 1906, under the *nom de plume* "Juvenal," decried the wanton and wasteful practices of lumbermen. Readers were informed that

> " . . . a 'market' is a log thirteen feet long and nine inches in diameter or its equivalent. In the old days nothing was cut under ten inches in diameter. This maintained the forest in some degree and permitted another crop. But the present 'four to one' method means that instead of timber the lumbermen are cutting poles of only about five inches average diameter. The pulp mill wants it all. . . . The same process is going on in other sections of the Adirondacks and the State cannot too rapidly push the acquisition of forest lands within the boundaries of the park."[5]

Conservationist Gifford Pinchot reinforced "Juvenal's" concerns in 1910. "The connection," he wrote, "between forests and rivers is like that between father and son. No forests, no rivers."

Logging practices seemed less severe prior to the 1920s than afterwards because the demands were different. Loggers tended to cause deterioration of the woods but not total devastation. In the Northeast, including the Adirondacks, the forest was resilient. Climate and soil were receptive to tree growth. Tree species were strong and vigorous, so much so that the forest stood considerable abuse. Where fire had not been the culprit, natural reproduction generally occurred, though it did not always produce the most desirable tree types. The cut-over lands failed to produce yields as high as they had before they were visited by lumberjacks, and damage was directly proportional to the harshness of the cutting methods practiced. The chief offenders were the pulpwood cutters, followed by the box board makers, chemical wood processors and fuel burners. Slash covered two-fifths of an area cut for these purposes and the remainder was a network of trails and logging roads. In the early days, there had been a more limited market for the small stuff, since the profit had been in bigger trees. The result was that, unlike the clear cutting method, the entire tree cover was seldom stripped at any one time.

Throughout the 1880s and 1890s the battle over New York's great wilderness heated up, fueled by changes in practices and what appeared to be drastic change in the land itself. Essentially, four points of view coalesced in the wake of the legislative enactments and constitutional change that fathered the Forest Preserve and Adirondack Park, promulgated by strong-minded, often well-financed groups. Among them were the advocates of preservation. Frequently well-to-do, many were part-time residents who wished the mountains frozen in time in order to perpetuate their beauty, healthfulness and recreational uniqueness. Often opposing the preservationists were those who conjured visions of excessive state control and saw in the intrusion of government the beginning of the end to the rights of property ownership and free enterprise. Then there were the new professionally-trained foresters. They preached conservation, controlled cutting, protection of the watershed and sustained income. Finally, there were the logging interests—owners and lumberjacks—who viewed the forest as a source of livelihood, and resented bitterly any imposition of control and restraint which inhibited the way they worked the woods. Somewhere in the middle ground, although sometimes forgotten, there were lumbermen who accepted and understood advances in scientific forestry, that forests might be managed and harvested to their long-term self interest. It was a belief which gained some early acclaim in the Adirondacks and some notoriety as well. To the present day, the issues and degree of agitation have remained much the same.

As the debate quickened and the public became more informed, a new player appeared on the field—the forest advocate. By America's centennial year of 1876, Judge Franklin B. Hough of Lowville had been lobbying hard for conservative logging practices in New York as well as before such august bodies as the American Association for the Advancement of Science. In 1876, he was appointed the first forestry agent in the U.S. Department of Agriculture and became the head of the Division of Forestry (forerunner to the present U.S. Forest Service) when it was created in 1881. He became the first official in the federal government charged with the oversight of forest resources. In 1886, Bernhard E. Fernow, another New Yorker (although born in Prussia), was appointed to the federal service. He was the first academically-prepared forester to go to Washington; he became the first director of the New York State College of Forestry founded at Cornell in 1898, a leading advocate of scientific forestry in America. And in 1893, Gifford Pinchot opened an office in New York City, gave himself the title of "consulting forester" and began a new profession.

Pinchot was born in 1865. After graduating from Yale in 1889, he went to Europe where he acquired first-hand knowledge of how the Old World managed its forests. In 1890, the year he returned to this country, "scientific forestry" was not really practiced publicly or privately anywhere in the United States. Setting aside public forest reserves and tree planting was not scientific forestry; nor was simply the preservation of natural forest areas. What Pinchot and his trained colleagues did was "to show Americans that real forestry aims to regulate the use of the axe rather than to stop it and seeks to promote forest development by natural reproduction rather than merely artificial planting." By 1892, Pinchot had promised George W. Vanderbilt a management plan for his Biltmore Forest near Asheville, North Carolina. The proposal included a detailed survey and cutting plan. He was assisted by a young lumberman, C. L. Whitney and his crew from Malone, New York. Pinchot did another plan for Vanderbilt in 1895 on the same principle. Neither was a great financial success, but the association gave him considerable exposure. Out of his first dealings with Vanderbilt came another project in 1892, this time with Vanderbilt's brother-in-law, W. Seward Webb.

The year Pinchot opened his New York office he began work as a consulting forester in the Adirondacks where he attempted to put in place the rudiments of scientific forestry within the state-owned Forest Preserve. Pinchot thought cutting on state land without the supervision of trained foresters would be disastrous. Simultaneously, there was an increasingly strong public sentiment against cutting timber of any kind. Preserving the beauty of the Adirondacks was becoming a common cause. In February 1894, William Fox, Superintendent of State Forests, invited Pinchot to speak in Albany to a high-powered gathering that included, among others, the American Forestry Association, the Adirondack Park Association, and the New York Forestry Association. Important people were present: J. Sterling Morton, Secretary of Agriculture and father of Arbor Day; Forester Bernhard E. Fernow; Pennsylvanian J. T. Rothrock; and influential New Yorkers including Morris K. Jessup and Warren Higbey, both deeply involved in the New York Forestry Association. It was Pinchot's first real chance to influence public policy and his subject was a good one: "Forester and Lumberman in the North Woods." (Pinchot later recalled the title as "Forester and Lumberman in the Adirondacks.") The essence of his paper was

> " . . . to distinguish *forestry* and *lumbering* and to show why the former was to be preferred for the general welfare of the State. In *lumbering,* he contended that there was concern only for getting the largest profit out of an existing forest crop, but in *forestry* there was interest in getting the largest return consistent with protecting and increasing the productive capacity of the forest."[6]

Pinchot's views were strongly endorsed. The public's feeling, however, was that there should be no cutting at all in the Adirondack wilderness. Managed forestry practices were considered inimical to the concept of "forever wild"; and, of course, the advocates of the latter view prevailed at the state's Constitutional Convention later that year in November 1894. Between 1894 and 1895, Pinchot first met and impressed New York Governor Teddy Roosevelt; began the study of the white pine woods of Franklin and Clinton counties in New York and in parts of Pennsylvania, with Henry S. Graves; and started to consider, as a career plan, becoming the Chief Forester of the United States. By 1896, he was appointed a member of the newly-established National Forest Commission.

That year, Pinchot also began a project in the Adirondacks that had lasting importance for private forestry in the north woods. The question was how to preserve and manage the spruce trees on the 40,000 acres of W. Seward Webb's Ne-Ha-Sa-Ne Park, a tract of land bordered on the east by Little Tupper Lake, on the west by Big Rock Lake, which included a part of the Beaver River's headwaters and was crossed by the Adirondack and St. Lawrence Railroad. It was land that had largely escaped the woodsman's axe and the consequences of serious forest fires. Pinchot's survey was completed in 1897 and "out of it came the formulation of a working plan which was to become a model for other American foresters." Noteworthy in the plan were a number of rules for cutting that gave the forest manager or forester authority to protect young growth, to safeguard against fire and to assess penalties against lumbermen for non-compliance. The Ne-Ha-Sa-Ne survey "also gave Pinchot data for a book which he titled *The Adirondack Spruce*. This was the first American book to give a detailed plan for the management of a particular forest, and was an important stimulus to the application of forestry principles to American conditions." The spruce was the most sought-after species for pulpwood processing; the book was widely read by Adirondack forest land owners.

Next to Ne-Ha-Sa-Ne Park was William C. Whitney's sixty-eight thousand acre tract. In 1898, Pinchot and his colleague Henry Graves undertook for the former Secretary of the Navy the same type of plan Pinchot had done for Dr. Webb. Both plans (as well as those done subsequently in the Adirondacks for such people as William Rockefeller, Ralph Brandreth, J. P. Morgan, The Moose River Lumber Company and later the Emporium Forestry Company) called for carefully prepared timber estimates and maps, contracts that prevented lumbermen from taking spruce under ten inches in diameter, and schedules for preserving some large trees for seed and the cutting without restriction of others for marketable timber. In 1900, Edward Burns, the estate manager at Ne-Ha-Sa-Ne, wrote Pinchot telling him, "I have heard only good words lately for cutting timber under forestry supervision as instituted by you, and I cannot imagine Dr. Webb going back to the old careless methods." He never did. In 1898, Pinchot was appointed the nation's chief forester and left New York for Washington. At age 33, he had inaugurated America's first efforts at experimental and scientific forestry; had been the catalyst for a new profession; and had written the first authoritative and professional studies on the growth and management of trees in public and private forests. It was a solid beginning in a new profession.

The nation's first scientific forester provided a firsthand account of the state of Adirondack logging in his treatise *The Adirondack Spruce*. According to Pinchot,

> " . . . lumbering, as at present practiced in the Adirondacks, affects the forest to its injury, because, in the first place, it decreases the number of valuable trees. The Spruce, which at best is only scattered here and there through the hardwoods, is removed, and no provision of any kind is made for its reproduction."

What the loggers left were "the hardwoods, the less valuable conifers—chiefly Hemlock and Balsam—and the defective spruce that cannot be used for pulp." Pinchot observed that "cutting for pulp does far more harm than cutting for lumber, because it takes a vastly greater number of trees." The standard methods were in and of themselves very harmful, mostly as a result of carelessness. Pinchot wrote:

> "Many young trees, where skidding is going on, lose pieces of their bark by contact with the harness or the logs, and afterward become unsound. Young trees of merchantable species are commonly cut to build skidways when it would be almost as easy to take less valuable kinds. In road-building the destruction of useful young growth is particularly noticeable. Young Spruce is often cut where other species are at hand and would answer the purpose just as well."

Forest fires and the clear cutting practices of the charcoal burners also spelled disaster. For example, when

> " . . . the forest is completely removed, as in places where Spruce occurs nearly pure or where the timber is cut for charcoal, the consequent drying up of the forest floor and washing of the soil has a decided and harmful influence on the flow of streams. The same result is brought about by the forest fires which have ravaged portions of the Adirondacks, and for the majority of which lumbering hitherto has been directly or indirectly responsible."

The basis for forest management was spelled out by Pinchot, but he made clear that

> " . . . it would be unfair to condemn all lumbering because the present method is not wholly right. The qualities of the Spruce, and the general circumstances which surround its utilization in the Adirondacks, make it plain that better methods are possible from every point of view. It is the purpose of practical forestry so to modify the present systems of cutting that the harm now done may be avoided and the removal of the old crop be of permanent benefit to the forest which remains. At the same time the question of revenue is kept prominently in view."[7]

Pinchot strongly believed that Adirondack land owners (other than the state) had to meet two conditions in order to successfully employ forest management. First, "the returns must be substantial enough to make it a profitable real property investment. Otherwise the lumbermen, most clubs, and nearly all private land owners will be unwilling to adopt it." And second, "the system of management must secure the establishment of a crop of trees to take the place of the timber cut, and it must improve the condition of the forest."

At Ne-Ha-Sa-Ne and everywhere else, the general rules which controlled conservative logging operations were, according to Pinchot:

1. Only trees marked by the forester must be cut, and each tree marked must be cut unless a reason satisfactory to the forester can be given for leaving it.

2. No timber outside the line of a road shall be used for corduroy, culverts, or other road purposes, until all timber cut for the clearing of the road has been utilized; and when more timber is necessary, all available trees of other kinds within reach must be used before any spruce is taken.

3. All lumber roads must be marked out by the contractor with the cooperation and assistance of the forester.

4. As a protection against fire all tops must be cut or lopped so that the thin branches will be brought in contact with the ground by the weight of the winter's snow.

5. Extreme care must be taken to prevent fire. No fire must ever be lighted where it can get into a rotten log or into the duff.

6. Great care must be taken not to injure young growth in felling timber, or to bark valuable young trees in skidding.

7. Felled trees must be cut into logs at once, to release young growth crushed by their fall, unless a reason satisfactory to the forester can be given for some other course.

8. Any young growth bent over by felled trees must be released and allowed to straighten without delay.

9. Provision for carrying out these regulations should be made in all contracts with lumbermen, and fines should be imposed by the contracts for failure to comply with them.[8]

In 1911, Pinchot surveyed the state of scientific forestry nationally and found that, despite all of his effort and good work, progress in the field had been modest at best. By this time he and Teddy Roosevelt were well on their way to establishing the National Progressive Party following in the wake of Pinchot's dismissal by President Taft as Chief Forester of the United States after his fight with Secretary of the Interior, Richard Ballinger. Speaking at the Hotel Astor in New York that year to the Camp Fire Club of America, Pinchot opened his remarks in characteristic style: "Forestry," he said, "is flourishing everywhere except in the woods." Presumably that got the audience's attention; if not, his reminder that the Adirondack forest was one of the state's "most precious possessions" must have. Why were these forest-covered mountains so important? Not just in supplying timber for an expanding market but perhaps more so as a water-flow resource, an unmatched recreation ground, "and as a vast sanitarium." In Pinchot's view, and that of many others, the Adirondack purchase was "probably the best investment the citizens of New York ever made." Everyone who had ever seen the Adirondacks from near or far either voiced an opinion as to their beauty and worth as a natural resource or saw in them the potential for easy exploitation. The occasions for sin had always been present.

Not all Adirondack lumbering operations were run by men of high principles and ideals. There was need for concern. Pinchot's converts were all too often outnumbered by the sinners. The Brooklyn Cooperage Company—a subsidiary of the Sugar Trust operating at Tupper Lake in the early years of the twentieth century—was a prime offender. Its practices were described as "needless and conscienceless vandalism." Pinchot himself stated forthrightly that the

> " . . . logging done by this company is more destructive than any other with which I am acquainted in the Eastern States, and the damage by the fires for which its carelessness is said to be responsible, will cost the people of New York large sums of money and long years of time to repair. . . . The Brooklyn Cooperage Company controls by ownership and lease 123,000 acres in the Adirondacks. Unless this organization is restrained by the strong hand of the State, every acre of that land will be despoiled of its forest growth and swept clean by fire."[9]

Not far from the destruction being wrought by the Cooperage Company was the Emporium Forestry Company at Conifer. Although it may have resembled a fiefdom, it was an enlightened one, prepared to accept new ideas about forestry. In 1910, at the beginning of its operations in the North Country, the Sykes and Gifford Pinchot worked out a cutting plan not unlike the one that had been tried at the Webb and Whitney tracts. It was for a one-square-mile experimental area, designed to demonstrate conservative logging, a model for the remainder of the Sykes holdings. "Only the ripe timber" was to be cut, "leaving sufficient seed trees to reforest the area, and using extreme care . . . not to injure or destroy any more young trees than is absolutely necessary." Clyde Sykes, writing to Austin Cary at the University of Minnesota in 1912, took pains to point out that Pinchot himself had "volunteered to go with us [the Sykes] and help us select just what trees are to be taken and whether or not the scheme will work out satisfactorily on a commercial basis." Pinchot's association with the Sykes family prompted him to remark, in contrast to his feeling about the Brooklyn Cooperage Company, that not all "Adirondack lumbermen as a body" were sinners. Quoting his friend W. L. Sykes, Pinchot noted with satisfaction that "the difference between conservative logging and forest destruction is that in the one case the timber land is an increasing asset, in the other a diminishing one." Pinchot had scarcely said it better himself a dozen years before. In a very real sense, this was the crux of the problem.

Nationally, Presidents Benjamin Harrison and Grover Cleveland had set aside millions of forested acres. Pinchot, through his consulting forestry business in New York and governmental career in Washington, had begun informing people of the need to protect the nation's natural resources. In 1898, the cumulative effort spurred the state legislature to charter the New York State College of Forestry at Cornell University with a curriculum which included timber physics, wood technology, forest history and politics, and forest management. By 1903, the college was discontinued; however, in 1911, the State College of Forestry at Syracuse University was founded to replace it. In 1912, the new college established the Ranger School at Wanakena, St. Lawrence County, and subsequently the demonstration forests at Cranberry Lake, Newcomb, and Warrensburg. Paul Smiths' College and its Department of Forestry soon followed.

In 1912, Hugh P. Baker, newly appointed dean of the Syracuse school, wrote a letter describing the organization of the college, its work and the help it required. First, Baker provided a brief history, explaining that

> "In 1898 the State Legislature established the New York State College of Forestry at Cornell University. For four years the College did very effective educational work under Dr. B. E. Fernow but owing to unfortunate circumstances arising from the management of lands in the Adirondacks, the College was closed in 1903. For several years, since the closing of the College of Forestry at Cornell, there has been an increasing feeling that the State should not be without a strong College of Forestry and in July, 1911, the Legislature by Special Act created the New York State College of Forestry at Syracuse University. The organic law of the College obligates it to carry on not only educational work at Syracuse University, a Ranger School in the Adirondacks, and among people throughout the State who may be interested

in our forests and their animal life, but requires that investigative work be carried on for the purpose of solving many important problems in connection with the protection and management of our forests and the reforestation of waste areas. To meet this last requirement a Forest Experiment Station of 100 acres is maintained just south of Syracuse."

Dean Baker also outlined the nature of the educational work. "The College has developed a five-year Professional Course; a one- and two-year Ranger Course given on the College Forest of 2,000 acres at Wanakena, N.Y., and a summer Camp of four weeks on Upper Saranac Lake. The Camp will be held for the first time during August 1913." The college needed good young men and the Dean solicited "the names of young men interested in a course in Forestry."[10]

In July 1919, the New York section of the Society of American Foresters held their second summer meeting at the Ranger School at Wanakena. The program included a brief history of the school, the purpose of which was

" . . . to turn out trained men to fill the gap between the technically trained Forester and the ordinary employee of the lumber industry or the guard or ranger in the forest. The value of a man trained under forest conditions to take charge of field work in forestry can hardly be estimated. It is no longer necessary for the lumbermen to select one from their employees who seems to be a little more promising than the others and laboriously train him to look after their interests in the field. The Ranger School does all this for him."[11]

It was a long time before the idea came to fruition, and the forester became installed as an integral part of the industry.

In addition to programmed propaganda for the cause of forestry, society members were told of the Ranger School's future plans, including "the erection of ample and substantial buildings and the enlargement of the student body. The establishment of a Woods Laboratory and Experiment Station where all sorts of forest investigations may be carried on." Society members were also taken to the north side of the college's forest and shown the various plantations made by Ranger School students.

"The Rich Lumber Company [had] operated on this area for soft woods and some hard woods. In 1908, a fire swept over the entire area, taking everything but a few swamp areas, since then other small fires have occurred. In 1912 this area was taken over by the School and a small amount of experimental planting was done up to and including

Spruce growing at the New York School of Foresters at Wanakena. Photograph by H. M. Beach.

Spruce seed at the New York State School of Foresters at Wanakena. Photograph by H. M. Beach.

W. L. Sykes, a Pinchot enthusiast, took a picture of natural reforestation near Conifer on the right-of-way of the Grasse River Railroad in 1932.

Gifford Pinchot's The Adirondack Spruce *published in 1898 influenced a generation of Adirondack lumbermen. He is seen here in 1893 in his capacity of "Consulting Forester" in his New York City office.*

1914. In 1914 a nursery was established. In 1915 the first section under the planting plan was planted. This plan has been followed consistently and was completed in the Spring of 1919."[12]

Forest management was not widely accepted in the Adirondacks until after 1910, the year Finch-Pruyn of Glens Falls hired a professional forester. There had been efforts by Webb and Whitney, followed by the Adirondack League Club, from the 1890s onward, and the early activities of the forestry schools. But Finch-Pruyn was the first major logging company in the North Country to institute such a program. Their forester's duties were precisely as Pinchot had recommended: make valuation surveys of company lands in the upper Hudson Valley aimed at greater selective cutting with trees taken lower on the stump; supervise the fire control system; and work in cooperation with the Conservation Department and U.S. Forest Service to study the growth rates of trees. Perhaps most important, he was to establish rotational cutting schedules. Ferris Meigs and the Santa Clara Lumber Company

> " . . . established a nursery for trees in its lot at Tupper Lake Junction about the year 1910, planted the seed, and the second year, transplanted into longer beds, and at four years planted in the woods what are called 'four year transplants.' . . . Later it was found that such trees could be purchased from the State of New York at $4.00 per thousand, and as the milling operations were moved to the Norwood property the nursery was abandoned. This was in 1916. A total of approximately one million trees were planted on their Racquette River lands by the Lumber Company. And though no profit was expected directly from this policy, indirect profit was secured in no mean measure."

The harsh view of the stereotypical logger or lumber baron as the great destroyer of forest resources soften in the light of Meigs' pronouncement that

> " . . . one of the foundation principles of the Company's treatment of the forest area was to exercise the most extreme care to cut the timber with the minimum of damage to the young growth. Taking only the larger trees was the unvarying rule. Cutting the trees close to the ground, another. Saving of, and protection to the young growth of conifers, another."[13]

Among Gifford Pinchot's earliest work was a plan for Santa Clara Lumber Company; its president Ferris Meigs had become a believer.

Finch-Pruyn and Santa Clara, both large logging companies employing a forester, understood clearly the reasons for professional management. At Conifer, the Sykes were also well aware that good forest practices protected their investment. In January 1912, W. L. Sykes wrote to Pinchot telling him how much he respected him as a man and for "the intense desire you show to preserve our forests and natural resources." But Sykes continued, "What I fear most now is that it will be impossible for us to harmonize the timber land and lumber manufacturing interests, and I think that they could be brought together." The momentum for better forestry was at a fairly high peak. The Sykes' Emporium, with other powers of the Adirondack logging community, were very important to the movement. On April 23, 1912, P. S. Dinsdale of Washington, D.C., executive secretary of the American Forestry Association, invited Clyde Sykes to a board of directors meeting of the association to be held at Lake Clear Junction "where the board and guests will view the New York State nurseries and plantations," and perhaps in the afternoon "go to Paul Smiths and see additional planting work."

The Conifer men were in demand. The proximity of the Sykes' operations at Conifer and Cranberry Lake to the Ranger School at Wanakena prompted Dean Baker of the College of Forestry to enlist their help almost immediately. In August 1912, he wrote to say that Syracuse had hired P. T. Coolidge, a graduate of Harvard and the "Yale Forest School," as a director of the Ranger School. Baker confided that "as he is nearby, I presume he will go over often and . . . with students." Later the same year, Nelson C. Brown, also of the parent college in Syracuse, wrote Sykes that he, together with some faculty and students, were going to visit Conifer in late December on a field trip.

> "What I want the boys to get is to become acquainted with the typical logging and milling operations. They will have an outline to follow and will be expected to work up a comprehensive report describing and showing the costs of each individual operation, such as felling and bucking, skidding, hauling, railroading, etc., etc."[14]

The educated forester/lumberman was a new breed in the years just before and following World War I. He wanted work, and business wanted him. The Emporium Forestry Company had written to A. B. Recknagel, forester and professor in the Department of Agriculture at Cornell, seeking names. Recknagel recommended William H. Doggett of Dedham, Massachusetts to Sykes, stating that Doggett "had technical training in Forestry at Cornell and Yale," and that on finishing at Yale in 1917, "he immediately enlisted in the Army and spent two years in Europe." He served with the 10th and 20th Engineers (Forestry) U.S. Army and for the most part was in charge of estimating and acquiring fuel wood and supervising the French and American soldier/laborers who cut it. Recknagel had told Doggett that the company he was applying to was "one of the largest timberland owners in the Adirondacks." Sykes wrote to Doggett that

> "The Emporium Lumber Company and the Emporium Forestry Company are now engaged in practical forestry in that we are holding considerably over 150,000 acres of land in the three states of New York, Pennsylvania and Vermont. That part of the land which we have cut over is for the most part reproducing timber, at least to a certain extent and a very good percentage of it has a very good stand of young thrifty trees."[15]

The position of forester at Emporium was still equivocal; he was not going to shape policy. He would work in the woods department of the firm and "have more or less to do with our executives in general forestry matters." What the company really wanted and preferred was a combination person, "a man of some practical lumber experience, particularly in woods work, with a college trained forester."

Since Pinchot's comment in 1911 about forestry flourishing everywhere except in the woods, there had been change and some progress. Yale, Harvard, the University of Michigan and others sent their students and came themselves to see the Sykes at Conifer. R. C. Hawley of the Yale Forestry School wrote in June 1912, from Big Moose where he and a group of students were camped "studying the forestry situation in the Adirondacks" because he had been told by C. R. Pettis, the New York State Forester, that he should visit Conifer's "woods operations and hardwood mill." They were "the most advanced ideas in the utilization of hardwoods" to be found anywhere. C. L. Hill from the University of Michigan's Department of Forestry wanted to place his students with Emporium for the summer since a number of them were New Yorkers who wished to work in their own state. "The only favor," Hill asked, was that the students "be given a chance at different kinds of work during the course of the summer, so as to get a little acquaintance with more than one side of it." Irving Bailey from Harvard's School of Forestry had been sending his students for the last several years to the Sykes' Pennsylvania works at Galeton. He now wished to have them go to Conifer for six weeks beginning January 2 or 3. Bailey, politically

sensitive, wanted Clyde Sykes to "understand . . . that no results prejudi-
cial to your concern arise from our visits to your operations. We are
merely studying general methods and efficiency and have only an inci-
dental interest in detail of work for any given locality." Forestry was
doing well in the universities and so was the Emporium Forestry Company.

By the 1920s, with the growth of theoretical and academic work at
the university level, knowledgeable individuals were beginning to think
in terms of a national timberland policy. The tendency of the times was,
it seemed, "unmistakably towards regulation and control of private enterprise." A. B. Recknagel stated the nature of the problem. Public ownership was always the *bête noir* of the businessman. It was acceptable to
Recknagel, however, particularly if it safeguarded the public's welfare.

> "In the case of forests it is ever necessary, because the very conditions
> of ownership are often adverse to the public interest. The private
> owner was often forced, because of financial obligations to himself and
> to his stockholders, to manage his forest contrary to the dictates of
> public interest. For example, if the national forests, instead of being
> run at a yearly deficit, were to be commercialized so as to show a
> profit the exigency might subject the Forest Service to exactly the
> same criticisms as those made against the private owner."[16]

This is the essence of most discussions on public land policy, even now.
It seemed "axiomatic that, in the older settled portions of the country at
least, the timberland owners realize that the timberland is their greatest
asset." Clearly most were "endeavoring to protect it from fire and to
maintain its productiveness." This was what the conservationists
wanted, but "the trouble comes in choosing the means to accomplish
this end."

Echoing what W. L. Sykes had been saying five years earlier, Recknagel pointed out in 1919 that "the vast majority of timberland owners"
felt there was a middle ground. It seemed clear, he added, that

> " . . . the interests of those who are consuming the wood and destroy-
> ing the forests are to a great extent identical with the interests and
> desires of those who would protect and enlarge the forests. The great-
> est problem of the near future will be bringing the apparently diverse
> interests together. . . ."[17]

This would not be easy nor would it happen quickly.

Recknagel lobbied, as always, for common sense and cooperation
among the contending factions. The problem was threefold:

"First, the measures of public and private forestry practice now in effect or in reasonable prospect are inadequate to guarantee the timber supply which the nation will require in the future. Second, if our remaining forests are to be saved and our wood-using industries are to prosper, the privately-owned timberland must be placed on a basis of continuous forest production. Third, the time is now come for the privately owned timberland to take its place in a national program of forestry."

The reconciling of conflicting interests seemed brighter if for no other reason than that public sentiment could be directed and changed. In the past, Recknagel pointed out,

" . . . public sentiment has, heretofore, largely contented itself with 'damning the lumbermen'—and with some justice, it must be admitted. But if the old era of private exploitation has definitely passed, so has the era of 'Woodsman spare that tree.' Public sentiment, properly directed, will prevent abuses in private business; not by a wholesale, destructive criticism of all private operators but only by an intelligent and helpful interest in the timber owner's problems."[18]

By the 1950s, there was some evidence that old antagonists had at least reached a modicum of accommodation.

Elwood R. Maunder of the Forest History Foundation interviewed A. B. Recknagel in Tucson, Arizona in October 1958, and his comments reinforce what had transpired in the Adirondacks. Maunder reminded Recknagel of the head-on collision that had occurred in the first two decades of the twentieth century between "the Pinchovian concept of forestry" with its "emotionally charged" public opinion in support of conservation and the *laissez-faire* capitalistic force of the nineteenth century lumber industry. This, plus considerable muckraking support, had assured prolonged conflict between the two groups. Recknagel agreed that the situation was slow to resolve itself since the two factions were "absolutely at logger heads until the depression." The Great Depression, bad as it was, brought many old foes together. "The greatest thing that Roosevelt did," Recknagel told Maunder, "was to put the National Recovery Act into effect," because it "embodied the famous Article X in the Lumber Code, the Conservation Code." For Recknagel, the 1930s were halcyon days for forestry in Washington, not equalled until the 1950s when there was a "renaissance of forestry." He went on to say,

"We have a happy combination right now—a renaissance of the idealistic attitude, but it is well tempered by the knowledge that forestry is also based on industrial support. And the combination, if it can be carried on to its ultimate end, will be the solution of our forestry problem. It will never be done by federal control. . . . There are a few die-hards that still believe in it, but . . . it can't be done by anything except the strong support of the American people."

What, asked Maunder in 1958, did the future hold for forestry? Recknagel replied,

"We still are very weak in the education of most of our foresters in what might be called industrial forestry, that is, there is a great lack of knowledge of the business aspect of forestry on the part of most of the foresters who've gone merely through the standard curriculum of the forest school. We learned it the hard way."

Nevertheless, Recknagel re-affirmed the great days of the New Deal and sadly told Maunder:

"When all this smoke finally cleared away and the NRA [National Recovery Administration] was abolished and we went back to our separate little organizations, I stayed on as secretary for a while at least with the Empire State Forest Products Association. But somehow the old spirit didn't exist that had been there before. So many of the older men had either died or had moved elsewhere, and their interests were more concentrated outside of New York. I'm sorry to say this, but the Empire State Forest Products Association today reminds me of a group of nostalgically-minded older men who come together twice a year to have a good dinner and to talk over old times. That's not a nice thing to say but that's about what it's like. Clyde Sykes you've heard of, haven't you—the Sykes of Pennsylvania? Clyde Sykes says that's all wrong. 'We're like a group of firemen sitting around playing checkers until the fire breaks out again.' "

Maunder also quizzed Recknagel about the strength of "the 'preservationist group' in the Adirondacks." Recknagel replied that they were very "strong in New York City." A veritable hotbed of it, suggested Maunder. "Well," said Recknagel, "it's because of the great wealth of the Adirondack landowners who center in New York City."

In retrospect, Recknagel was fortunate. He saw it all happen and was part of most of it. He told Elwood Maunder with considerable satisfaction and pride that

" . . . those foresters who've been fortunate like myself not only to live through the early period and can now see this great future development already taking shape can feel that their lives were indeed not wasted. . . . We've made one serious error, of course, and that's in so long deferring the cooperation between industry and forestry. . . . Today [1958] it's a real pleasure to see right here at this meeting lumbermen who are hobnobbing and friendly and understanding of the forestry problems, and rabid conservationists who are hobnobbing with lumbermen whom they wouldn't even have set down to eat with in the early days, and they both are working for the same end."[19]

In a very real sense, the rise of conservative forestry and forest management parallels the Emporium Forestry Company's history in the Adirondacks from its beginnings around 1910 through 1950. Despite hard words and a continuous ebb and flow of public opinion, the New York State Department of Environmental Conservation, the Society of American Foresters, the Empire State Forest Products Association, forest landowners and industrialists—through occasional enforced cooperation—came to the understanding that New York's woodlands were a most valuable and, above all, renewable resource. If logging was to continue, then it would have to be well planned so as to benefit the total culture of the region—forests, land, wildlife, water resources and people. Forest managers and harvesting contractors (jobbers) subscribed to a set of Pinchovian guidelines that years earlier would have been thought impossible to suggest, let alone follow. By the 1970s, after years of patient negotiating, everyone agreed to

" . . . keep stream crossings to a minimum and plan them carefully; protect stream banks by controlling skidding and felling close to the stream; plan carefully the protection of slopes exceeding 30 percent; properly locate, design and build all roads and skid trails, select landing locations that avoid erosion problems; comply with New York's woodland fire laws, exercise care to maintain landscape qualities along major travel corridors; and wherever possible keep landings out of sight and dress up landings and access roads after use."[20]

The procession of a region away from near total exploitation toward a future of hope and preservation is encapsulated in the words of a man whose business was logging. W. L. Sykes, in 1936, never one to romanticize after thirty years of Adirondack lumbering wrote to a colleague:

"I want you to slow up at several points after leaving North Creek and Indian Lake and Blue Mountain Lake and Long Lake, as these points are in the heart of the Adirondacks where you will see some beautiful mountain scenery and enough virgin timber to make you want to stop to build a sawmill."

But he accepted the inevitable, and without any editorial comment, Sykes concluded his letter by stating "most of it is owned by the state and they are not permitted under the Constitution to cut a tree."[21] A balance had been reached, an equilibrium, if you will, among the logging interests, the preservationists, the tourists and the state.

In a political world, no one is ever completely satisfied. One thing seems certain: for the present, ownership of the forest is now so diversely contested that its future is assured. This will remain the case so long as controls are maintained and so long as each of the using factions can be assured an equitable piece of the forest pie. Converts and sinners of an earlier day have found salvation but neither group is secure about how long it will last. The reader should bear in mind William Cronon's words in *Changes in the Land: Indians, Colonists and the Ecology of New England*, 1983: "There has been no timeless wilderness in a state of perfect changelessness, no climax forest in permanent stasis." Neither has there been any such condition in Adirondack logging, the Adirondack landscape, nor the larger Adirondack community with its diverse people and ideas.

Endnotes

Chapter One: Men and Machines in the Forest

1   *New York Lumber*, 15 January 1905, p. 11.

2   Lee J. Vance, "Lumbering in the Adirondacks," *Godey's Magazine*, March 1896, pp. 229-231.

3   Nelson T. Samson, "Woods Labor in the Adirondacks," (diss., Syraucse, N.Y., State University of New York College of Forestry, 1952), p. 69, 72.

4   J. D. Gilmour, *Logging, Past and Future*, (Montreal, 1936) p. 1-2.

5   G. W. Sykes to First Citizens Bank & Trust Co., Utica, N.Y., 16 February 1934. Emporium Forestry Company Records, Box 98. (Hereafter referred to as E.F.C.R.)

6   C. W. Mason, "The Coming of the Tractor," *Lumber Camp News*, May 1949, p.12. See also Floy S. Hyde, *Adirondack Forests, Fields and Mines* (Lakemont, N.Y., North Country Books, 1974), p. 59. Hyde states that Gould acquired its first three Linn tractors in 1918-19. Mason's account in *Lumber Camp News* assigns a slightly earlier date. The same journal in September 1954 states that heavy steam-powered Lombard tractors were used around Inlet in the early 1900s.

7   O. F. Edwards to the Holt Manufacturing Company, May 1919. E.F.C.R. Box 13. The most recent article on tractors and logging is James A. Young and Jerry D. Budy, "Adaptation of Tracklaying Tractors for Forest Road and Trail Construction," *Journal of Forest History*, vol. 31 (July 1987), pp.122-132. The Holt Tractor Company of Stockton, California merged with C. L. Best Tractor Company of San Leandro in 1925 to form the Caterpillar Tractor Company. See Reynold M. Wik, "Benjamin Holt and the Invention of the Track-type Tractor," *Technology and Culture*, vol. 20 (January 1979), pp. 90-107; and his *Benjamin Holt and Caterpillar: Tracks and Combines* (St. Joseph, Michigan, American Society of Agricultural Engineers, 1948).

8   Paul C. Perkins, "Effect of Mechanized Logging on Forestry Management," *The Northern Logger and Timber Processor*, May 1969, p. 22.

9   "Skidders Versus Horses," *The Northern Logger . . .*, September 1981, p. 3. See also Douglas B. Monteith and David W. Taber, compilers, "Profile of New York Loggers," *Report No. 38*, (Syracuse, N.Y., Applied Forestry Research Institute, February 1979), p. 16.

10 Fred C. Simmons, *Northeastern Loggers' Handbook*, (Washington, D.C., U.S. Dept. of Agriculture, 1951), p. 147.

11 *First Annual Report of the Forest Commission of the State of New York for the Year 1885* (Albany, State of New York, 1886), pp. 48-49. See also "Adirondack Lumbering," *The St. Lawrence Plain Dealer* (Canton, N.Y., 27 March 1980) for account of preparations for drive.

12 *Ibid.*, p. 48.

13 Vance, "Busy Times in the Adirondacks," *Harper's Weekly*, 27 February 1892, p. 214.

14 See account by E. A. MacDonald as quoted in Watson B. Berry, "A North Country Chronicle," *Farm and Garden*, December 1955.

15 Ferris J. Meigs, "The Santa Clara Lumber Company, 1888-1938," vol. 1 (typescript, n.p., 1941), pp. 78, 80-82. Adirondack Museum Library.

16 Pete Fosburgh, "The Big Boom," *New York State Conservationist*, April-May 1947, p. 16. The reminiscences of Yankee John Galusha of Minerva are quoted by Hochschild, *Township 34*, p. 81.

17 "Four Spring Drives Under Way in Adirondacks and Tug Hill," *Lumber Camp News*, May 1940, p. 3.

18 *Ibid.*

19 *Ibid.*

20 "Tupper Lake Lumbermen Recall Spring Log Drives of Bygone Years" [from *Tupper Lake Free Press*], *Lumber Camp News*, May 1946.

21 *Lumber Camp News*, May 1950, p. 4.

22 Simmons, *Northeastern Loggers' Handbook*, p. 17.

23 "Brown Company Yarding Crews Use Power Chain Saws," *Lumber Camp News*, May 1950, p. 4.

24 *Ibid.* See also "Mechanized Logging Increased in Northeast," *Lumber Camp News*, March 1947.

25 Charles Hines, "Case Histories of Integrated Logging Operations / Integrated Hardwood Logging," *Northern Logger*, July 1963, p. 15.

26 Frances E. Smalley, "From Oxen to Arches," *Northern Logger*, April 1953, p. 7.

Chapter Two: Emigrés From Pennsylvania

1 "Inventory of Personal Property" sold by George McCoy and Sons to the Emporium Lumber Company, 9 January 1911. E.F.C.R. Box 2; see also G. W. Sykes to Howard Hanlon, 9 January 1958. E.F.C.R. Box 1.

2 "Articles of Agreement between the Emporium Lumber Company and A. A. Low," 30 December 1910. E.F.C.R. Box 4.

3 W. L. Sykes to G. W. Sykes, 31 July 1912. E.F.C.R. Box 5.

4 "Articles of Agreement between the Emporium Lumber Company and McClinton", E.F.C.R. Box 4.

5 J. D. Gilmour, *Logging Past and Future* (Montreal, Canadian Pulp and Paper Association, 1936), p. 2.

6 William F. Fox, *History of the Lumber Industry in the State of New York (1614-1900)* (Harrison, N.Y., Harbor Hill, 1976), pp. 62, 65. Originally published in *Sxith Annual Report of the Forest, Fish and Game Commission of the State of New York* (Albany, State of New York, 1901). Subsequently published in *Bureau of Forestry Bulletin No. 34* (Washington, D.C., U.S. Dept. of Agriculture, 1902).

7 As quoted in Floy S. Hyde, *Adirondack Forests, Fields and Mines*, (Lakemont, N.Y., North Country Books, 1974), pp. 40-41.

8 E.F.C.R. Box 1.

9   W. L. Sykes to Frank Greco, 9 May 1912. E.F.C.R. Box 1.

10   "Brochure," The Grasse River Railroad Corporation, c. 1921. E.F.C.R. Box 204.

11   W. L. Sykes to A. C. Stewart, 10 April 1918. E.F.C.R. Box 204.

12   "Broadside," dated 12 May 1916, Grasse River Railroad Corporation, E.F.C.R. Box 1.

13   Certificate of Incorporation of Emporium Forestry Company," E.F.C.R. Box 1.

14   W. C. Sykes to Utica Office, Emporium Forestry Company, 30 January 1924. E.F.C.R. Box 1.

15   G. W. Sykes, "Emporium Forestry Company History," (typescript, Conifer, n.d. [c. 1950].) E.F.C.R. Box 1.

16   Statement probably prepared by W. C. Sykes, c. 1939. E.F.C.R. Box 1.

17   Internally dated 1938, in E.F.C.R. Box 2. In September 1945 the 50,000 acres of this tract were sold to the Draper Corporation whose mill in Tupper Lake produced bobbins and lumber stock.

18   William S. Gove, "William L. Sykes and the Emporium, Part III," *The Northern Logger and Timber Processor*, December 1970. See also "Emporium Forestry Mill Changes Hands," *Lumber Camp News*, May 1949, p. 1. Heywood-Wakefield had been leasing the Emporium plant since 1946-47.

Chapter Three: Diversity Among the Pines

1   A. B. Recknagel, *The Forests of New York* (New York, Macmillan, 1923), p. 34.

2   Douglas B. Monteith and David W. Taber, compilers, "Profile of New York Loggers," *Report No. 38*, (Syracuse, N.Y., Applied Forestry Research Institute, February 1979), p. 3.

3   For prices and comparative costs see J. J. Slattery to Emporium Lumber Company, 15 October 1912. E.F.C.R. Box 8. See also "Inventory of Conifer Inn," 31 December 1919, Box 8; "Conifer Mill Pay Roll," May 1911, Box 4; and W. C. Sykes to John R. Campbell, 24 June 1912, Box 5.

4   S. H. Conners to Emporium Forestry Company, 30 April 1919. E.F.C.R. Box 9.

5   Ferris J. Meigs, "The Santa Clara Lumber Company, 1888-1938," vol. I (typescript, n.p., 1941), pp. 83-86. Adirondack Museum Library.

6   Sheila Arsenault Hutt, "An Adirondack Lumberjack: Romeo L. Arsenault," (typescript, n.p., 1975), pp. 9, 13. Adirondack Museum Library.

7   Robert D. Bethke, *Adirondack Voices: Woodsmen and Woods Lore* (Urbana, Ill., University of Illinois Press, 1981), p. 23.

8   Horace Greeley, *et. al., The Great Industries of the United States* (Hartford, 1872), p. 821.

9   William McLoughlin, *A Short History of Logging at Lake Ozonia* (typescript, n.p., 1977), p. 12. Adirondack Museum Library.

10   Reed, *Lumberjack Sky Pilot*, pp. 63-64, 66. See also employees' letter to W. C. Sykes, 7 March 1921, E.F.C.R. Box 132.

11   *Lumber Camp News*, February 1951 and January 1952.

12   Ferris J. Meigs, "The Santa Clara Lumber Company . . ." vol. I, pp. 84-85.

13   Eric Bleicken, "The High Lead Story," *The Northeastern Logger*, May 1963, p. 46.

14   William B. Marleau, *Big Moose Station: A Story From 1893 to 1983* (Big Moose, N.Y., Marleau Family Press, 1986), p. 290.

15   "Old Lumbermen," *Lumber Camp News*, May 1952, p. 23.

16 Bleicken, "The High Lead Story," *The Northeastern Logger*, May 1963, p. 46.

17 "John Davignon Dies at Tupper Lake Oct. 9," *Lumber Camp News*, November 1949, p. 4.

18 Nelson T. Samson, "Woods Labor in the Adirondacks, (diss., State University of New York College of Forestry, Syracuse, 1952), pp. 58, 94, 104-105.

19 George Fowler, "Wood Cutters—A Shortage," *Northern Logger*, August 1973, p. 24.

Chapter Four: The Realities of Utopia

1 See Alfred Truman's description of a visit to Conifer (typescript, c. 1917) in E.F.C.R. Box 1. Adirondack Museum Library.

2 *Ibid.*

3 *Ibid.*

4 *Ibid.*

5 W. T. Turner to Chester Sykes, 21 October 1920 and W. C. Sykes to W. L. Sykes, 19 October 1920. E.F.C.R. Box 15.

6 W. T. Turner to George H. Bowers, Esq., 21 October 1920. E.F.C.R. Box 15.

7 W. L. Sykes to W. C. Sykes, 8 Novermber 1920. E.F.C.R. Box 15.

8 William B. Marleau, *Big Moose Station* (Big Moose, N.Y., Marleau Family Press, 1986), p. 331.

9 Frank A. Reed, *Lumberjack Sky Pilot* (Old Forge, N.Y., North Country Books, 1965), p. 100.

10 *Ibid.*, p. 10.

11 Harold K. Hochschild, *Township 34*, (New York, privately published, 1952), p. 111.

12 Sheila Arsenault Hutt, "An Adirondakc Lumberjack: Romeo L. Arsenault," (typescript, n.p., 1975), p. 9. Adirondack Museum Library.

13 Herbert Keith, *Men of the Woods* (Blue Mountain Lake, Adirondack Museum, 1972), p. 157.

14 Ferris J. Meigs, "The Santa Clara Lumber Company, 1888-1938," vol. 1 (typescript, n.p., 1941), pp. 23-24. Adirondack Museum Library.

15 Clyde Sykes to H. M. Ingraham, 23 October 1919. E.F.C.R. Box 1.

16 *Watertown Daily Standard*, Watertown, N.Y. July 1920 (typescript of newspaper article, in E.F.C.R. Box 15).

17 W. L. Sykes to New York Civic League, 19 October 1920. E.F.C.R. Box 15.

18 New York Civic League to W. L. Sykes, 4 December 1920. E.F.C.R. Box 15. That the Sykes were dedicated non-drinkers was perfectly clear from a letter Clyde Sykes wrote to the Retail Credit Company on January 6, 1931 stating that officers and members of the firm were "all total abstainers from liquor." E.F.C.R. Box 15.

19 Marleau, *Big Moose Station . . .*, p. 216.

20 Mrs. Sid Lyon to W. C. Sykes, 3 August 1920. E.F.C.R. Box 15, and unsigned and undated letter to Clyde Sykes, E.F.C.R. Box 132.

21 Mrs. John R. North to the Emporium Forestry Company, 20 February 1935. E.F.C.R. Box 132 and Mrs. E. Day to Clyde Sykes, 23 October 1920. E.F.C.R. Box 15.

22 Reed, *Lumberjack Sky Pilot*, p. 23, and Will L. Erhard to George Sykes, 19 May 1920. E.F.C. R.

23   W. C. Sykes to Dr. E. H. Joy and Bishop William Hunt, 24 april 1919. E.F.C.R. Box. 12.

24   Floy S. Hyde, *Adirondack Forests, Fields and Mines* (Lakemont, N.Y., North Country Books, 1974), p. 41.

25   Reed, *Lumberjack Sky Piolt*, pp. 78-79. See also, Aaron Maddox, Lantern Slide Lecture Notes, Adirondack Museum accession files, in which he describes one of the mission's preachers using a Ford, another a motorcycle, and wishing for another Ford and even a motorboat to visit the 150 camps "preaching in schoolhouses, railroad stations, hotels and in the open air." This was in November 1917.

26   George Parrotte to Mr. and Mrs. [Clyde] Sykes, 3 January 1943. E.F.C.R. Box 132.

Chapter Five: The Hazards of Woods Work

1   Daniel Ward, "Environmental Perception and Folk Outlook," (n.p., 1976), p. 67; also Robert Bethke, *Adirondack Voices: Woodsmen and Woods Lore* (Urbana, Ill., University of Illinois Press, 1981), p. 141.

2   W. L. Sykes to Dudley Dorr, 3 February 1919. E.F.C.R., Box 13, Adirondack Museum Library. In Saranac Lake the pioneer work for improving the workplace environment and hence workers' health and safety was carried on by Dr. LeRoy Gardner in the 1920s and '30s.

3   W. L. Sykes to Institute for Crippled and Disabled Men, 30 December 1920. E.F.C.R. Box 8.

4   "Form C-2, State Industrial Commission," 1920. E.F.C.R. Box 9. See also David M. Ellis, *et al*, *Short History of New York State* (Ithaca, Cornell University Press, 1967, revised edition), pp. 536-537.

5   W. Clyde Sykes to Cyrus W. Phillips, 4 February 1919, E.F.C.R., Box 8, and F. C. Thompson to Emporium Forestry Company, 2 May 1919. E.F.C.R. Box 8.

6   W. J. Snyder to W. L. Sykes, 8 January 1918. E.F.C.R. Box 202; Memorandum to File by W. L. Sykes, 7 May 1918. Box 203.

7   G. W. Sykes to Lumber Mutual Casualty Insurance Company, 19 May 1927. E.F.C.R. Box 72. Henry Dean's sworn statement on the death of John Macey, May 18, 1927. E.F.C.R. Box 72. This box contains Emporium Forestry Company accident reports from 1921 to 1931.

8   Frank A. Reed, *Lumberjack Sky Pilot* (Old Forge, N.Y., North Country Books, 1965), pp. 76-77.

9   "Woodsman in Hospital After Cigarette Sets Mattress Ablaze," *Lumber Camp News*, February 1950, p. 8.

10   "Lumbering Program Makes Many Changes," *Ibid.*, December 1949, p. 34.

11   ". . . Flown to New York for Treatment," *Ibid.*, April 1952, p. 23.

12   Harold K. Hochschild, *Township 34* (New York, privately published, 1952), pp. 242, 346, 387-390. See also *The New York Times*, 2 December 1910; and Charles E. North, M.C., "An Investigation of Recent Outbreaks of Typhoid Fever in an Adirondack Camp, and the Discovery of a Typhoid Carrier," *Medical Record*, 25 March 1911, quoted in full as Appendix V of Hochschild, pp. 549-555.

13   W. C. Sykes to W. L. Sykes, 11 January 1921. E.F.C.R. Box 76.

14   W. C. Sykes to Dr. Herman F. Senftner, 11 Janaury 1921. E.F.C.R. Box 76.

15   Herman Senftner to W. C. Sykes, 15 January 1921. E.F.C.R. Box 76.

16   Clyde Sykes to Dr. Senftner, 12 March 1921. E.F.C.R. Box 76, and *Ibid.*, 19 January 1921.

17   Francis Cantwell to the Emporium Forestry Company, 19 August 1921, E.F.C.R. Box 76.

18   *Ibid.*

19   *Ibid.*

20   W. C. Sykes to the Honorable E. J. Jones, 24 August 1921. E.F.C.R. Box 76. *Watertown Daily Times*, 27 February 1923. In these years, influenza was a frightening word. In 1918-1919 there had been a great pandemic which resulted in 21 million deaths throughout the world, nearly one half million in the United States. There had been earlier flu epidemics in the U.S., one in 1789 and another in 1889-1890, also pandemic in scope. It was not until 1933 that Smith, Andrews, and Laidlaw in the United Kingdom isolated the filterable virus which caused influenza. See Bordley and Harvey, *Two Centuries of American Medicine . . . ,* pp. 214-215.

21   Clyde Sykes letter to newspapers, all between 10-15 March 1923. E.F.C.R. Box 76; also Harold Johnson to Clyde Sykes, 21 March 1923. E.F.C.R. Box 76.

22   Nelson T. Samson, "Woods Labor in the Adirondacks" (diss., State University of New York College of Forestry, Syracuse, 1952), pp. 88-93. Writing in the March 1952 issue of *Lumber Camp News*, John W. Stock of Conifer stated that "logging has by far the greatest number" of lost time accidents. "The record shows that woods work is the most dangerous occupation for an American worker."

23   Horace Greeley, *et al, Great Industries of the United States* (Hartford, 1872), p. 823.

Chapter Six: The Woods Ablaze

1   *Annual Report of the Forest Commission For the Year 1894*, (Albany, State of New York, 1895), pp. 11, 13.

2   A. B. Recknagel, *The Forests of New York* (New York, Macmillan, 1923), pp. 61-64.

3   *Eighth and Ninth Reports of the Forest, Fish and Game Commission of the State of New York* [for years 1902 and 1903], (Albany, State of New York, n.d.), p. 102.

4   *Eighth and Ninth Reports . . . ,* pp. 106-107.

5   *Ibid.,* pp. 107-108.

6   *Ibid.,* p. 109.

7   *Ibid.,* pp. 110-111.

8   *Ibid.,* pp. 111-114.

9   Recknagel, p. 149. The causes of fire in the Adirondacks in 1921 broke down as follows:

Causes	Number of Fires	Acres Burned
Smokers	184	2,067
Locomotives	98	372
Fishermen	116	9,078
Campers	66	5,230
Lightning	47	202
Burning Brush	25	574
Berry Pickers	18	1,085
Hunters	20	1,522
Incendiary	13	3,318
Buring buildings	14	20
Lumberjacks	12	176
Children	8	9
Burning Rubbish	4	40
Totals	**633**	**23,743**

10 Recknagel, p. 67. A similar table for 1919, 1920 and 1921 yields the following information:

Number of Fires

Cause	1919	1920	1921
Locomotive	44	95	127
Smokers	77	81	212
Fishermen	35	54	118
Hunters	9	51	26
Campers	24	30	66
Incendiary	12	16	17
Burning Brush	15	15	38
Berry Pickers	21	9	23
Lightning	13	8	47
Children	2	8	9
Burning buildings	4	5	16
Blasting	—	2	—
Burning Rubbish	4	1	6
Lumberjacks	3	1	12
Sawmill	—	1	—
Steam roller or tractor	2	1	1
Fire balloon & fireworks ..	1	—	1
Bee hunters	—	—	4
Transmission line, burning auto, boiling sap	—	—	3
Totals	**266**	**378**	**726**

11 *Eighth and Ninth Reports . . .* , p. 124.

12 *Ibid.*, p. 125.

13 *Ibid.*, pp.126-127.

14 *Ibid.*, pp. 127-128.

15 *Ibid.*, pp. 129-130.

16 *Ibid.*, pp. 129-133.

17 *Ibid.*, p. 138.

18 William O'Brien to the Emporium Lumber Company, 13 January 1912. E.F.C.R. Box 5.

19 Memorandum of Record between C. R. Pettis and the Emporium Forestry Company, undated. E.F.C.R. Box 16. Also see April 21, 1919, Clyde Sykes wrote W. G. Howard, Assistant Superintendent of State Forests, E.F.C.R. Box 9. Also Emporium Forestry Company to Vitale and Rothery, 16 Nov. 1912. E.F.C.R. Box 8.

20 W. Clyde Sykes to Utica Office, 6 February 1920. E.F.C.R. Box 15. Also, W. C. Sykes to Retail Credit Company, 6 January 1931. E.F.C.R. Box 1.

21 W. L. Sykes to A. B. Recknagel, 10 July 1920. E.F.C.R. Box 15.

22 W. L. Sykes to F. P. and C. W. Sykes, 30 December 1920. E.F.C.R. Box 15.

23 W. L. Sykes to Ellwood Wilson, 30 March 1922. E.F.C.R. Box 15.

24 W. Clyde Sykes to H. K. Cortright, 27 May 1920. E.F.C.R. Box 15.

Chapter Seven: Conservative Forestry: An Epilogue

1   See "Clearcutting in the Adirondack Park," *Report of the Joint Government-Industry Steering Committee on Intensive Timber Harvesting in Adirondack Park* to the Adirondack Park Agency, May 1981 (Ray Brook, N.Y., 1982), p. 18. In 1887, the Forest Commission reported "We have cut and burned our forests with reckless wastefulness. . . . We h ave consumed our patrimony with spend-thrift prodigality." *Second Annual Report of the Forest Commission of the State of New York For the Year 1886* (Albany, 1887), p. 84.

2   William F. Fox, *History of the Lumber Industry in the State of New York (1614-1900)* (Harrison, N.Y., Harbor Hill, 1976), p. 8. Originally published in *Sixth Annual Report of the Forest, Fish and Game Commission of the State of New York* (Albany, 1901). Subsequently published in *Bureau of Forestry Bulletin No. 34* (Washington, D.C., U.S. Dept. of Agriculture, 1902).

3   *Annual Report of the New York Forest Commission for the Year 1893* (Albany, State of New York, 1894), p. 6.

4   March, 1896, p. 234.

5   Juvenal, "Lumbering in the Adirondacks," *Forest and Stream*, December 15, 1906, p. 939.

6   Harold T. Pinkett, "Gifford Pinchot, Consulting Forester, 1893-1898," *New York History*, vol. 39 (January 1958), p. 34.

7   Gifford Pinchot, *The Adirondack Spruce: A Study Of The Forest In Ne-Ha-Sa-Ne Park, With Tables of Volume and Yield and a Working-Plan for Conservative Lumbering* (New York, 1898), pp. 31-34.

8   *Ibid.*, pp. 112-113. Also, for the impact nationally of Pinchot's work, see Pinkett, *Gifford Pinchot: Private and Public Forester* (Urbana, Ill., University of Illinois Press, 1970).

9   Pinchot, "Address to the Camp Fire Club of America," 2 December 1911. Press release dated December 3 in E.F.C.R. Box 2. This speech was published in *Field and Stream*, vol. 16 (January, 1912).

10   "Announcement," New York State College of Forestry at Syracuse, 1912. E.F.C.R. Box 9. See also Louis C. Curth, *The Forest Rangers: A History of the New York State Ranger Force, 1885-1985.* (Albany, New York State Department of Environmental Conservation, 1987).

11   "Program" for the second summer meeting, New York State Section of the Society of American Foresters, July 29-31, 1919. Wanakena, New York. E.F.C.R. Box 9.

12   *Ibid.*

13   Ferris J. Meigs, "The Santa Clara Lumber Company, 1888-1938," vol. I (typescript, n.p., 1941), pp. 94-95. Adirondack Museum Library.

14   Nelson Brown to W. C. Sykes, 3 December 1912. E.F.C.R. Box 5.

15   George Sykes to W. H. Doggett, 10 January 1920. E.F.C.R. Box 14.

16   A. B. Recknagel, "A Permanent Timberland Policy for the U.S.," reprinted from *Lumber World Review* (10 April 1919). E.F.C.R. Box 13.

17   *Ibid.*

18   *Ibid.*

19   Elwood R. Maunder, Interview of A. B. Recknagel at Tucson, Arizona, 28 October 1958, Forest History Foundation, Inc., pp. 26-44.

20   See *New York State Environment* (December, 1975).

21   W. L. Sykes to W. H. Lear, 11 July 1936. E.F.C.R. Box 132.

Index

A.C. Lamb and Sons, 29, 30
A. Sherman Lumber Co., 26, 49, 68
Adirondack and St. Lawrence Railroad, 161
Adirondack League Club, 22, 140, 170
Adirondack Lodge, 134, 135
Adirondack Park, 129, 159
Adirondack Park Association, 161
Aldrich, Fred, 125
Allen, Dr. I.A., 120-122
Allen, William H., Jr., 95
American Bible Society, 98
American Forestry Association, 161, 171
American Pulpwood Association, 107, 109, 110, 116, 117
American Steamship Co., 34
Ames, Byron, 140
Andrus-Robinson Co., 50
Armour and Co., 72
Arsenault, Arthur, 21
Arsenault, Romeo, 71, 93
Arsenault, Thomas, 21
Ashlaw, Ted (Eddie), 14, 72
Atlantic Monthly, 84
Ausable Chasm, 135
Ausable Forks, 135
Ausable River, 156
Austin, Pa., 35, 60
Bailey, Irving, 172
Baker, Frank, 122
Baker, Dean Hugh, 166, 167, 171
Ballinger, Richard, 164
Beach, H.M., 99
Beaver Brook, 21
Beaver River, 140, 161
Beeman, Lyman A., 31
Bellamy, Edward, 88
Bellevue Medical Center, 114
Bell Telephone Company, 138, 144
Benzinger, Pa., 34, 60
Bernier, Elmer, 20, 22
Bethke, Robert C., 14, 71, 72, 93
Bewman Tannery, 152
Big Moose, 92, 140, 141, 172
Big Moose Lake, 131
Big Rock Lake, 161
Big Tupper Lake, 16, 154
Bird's Boat Livery, 31
Bishop, Olin S., 94

Blackwood's, 84
Blue Mountain Lake, 16, 93, 120, 122, 176
Bog River sawmill, 36, 37
Bolshevik, 69
Boonville, 88, 91
Boreas River, 15, 20, 21
Bowers, Charles E., 64
Bowers, George H, Esq., 91
Boyer, Eugene, 30
Bragdon, Henry W., 50
Brandreth Lake, 83
Brandreth, Ralph, 162
Brewster, B.R., 135
Brighton, 139
Broadwell, C.M., 30
Bronner, J.C., 64
Brooklyn Cooperage Co., 134, 165, 166
Brookville, Pa., 86
Brown, Nelson, 28, 171
Brownless, Louis, 122
Bureau of Workmen's Compensation, 106
Bureau Ponds, 21
Burns, Edward, 162
Burrill Saw and Tool Works, 29, 30
Burt, Bishop William, 98
Caflisch, William, 35, 63, 143
Caird, James, 123
Camp Eagle Nest, 120, 122
Cantwell, Francis Barry, 123
Carlson, C.W., 47
Carpenter, Russ, 20
Carr, Chester, 141
Carthage, 1, 141
Cary, Prof. Austin, 3, 165
Case, W.A. and Son, 46
Cedar River, 15, 21
Chateaugay Iron and Ore Co., 134
Chateaugay Railroad, 130, 141
Chesterfield, 135
Childwold, 47, 54, 72, 138
Childwold Station, 36, 47, 87, 89, 111, 122, 144
Chittenden, L.E., 16, 85, 157, 158
Churchill, F.M., 69
Clark Brothers, 36
Clayburg, 82
Clearwater, 131
Cleveland, Grover, 166
Clintonville, 157

Cohen, Dr., 112, 121, 122, 125
Commission of State Parks, 155
Conde Hardware Co., 46
Conifer, 1, 3, 5, 34, 35, 42-44, 46-51, 53, 54, 57, 59-61, 66, 69, 86, 87-91, 95, 96, 98, 99, 101, 106, 111, 112, 120-123, 125, 142, 144-146, 165, 169, 172
Conifer Boarding House, 122
Conifer Inn, 34, 44, 59
Conservation Commission (NYS), 143, 144
Conservation Law, 129
Coolidge, P.T., 171
Cranberry Lake, 47-50, 54, 60, 61, 87, 88, 90, 91, 95, 96, 111, 125, 126, 141, 143, 146, 166, 171
Croghan, 140
Cronon, William, 177
Crooked Lake, 22
Cutting, Frank A., 72
Dannemora, 135
D'Avignon, John, 82, 83
Dean, Henry, 112
Delaware & Hudson Railroad, 135
Derrick, 83
Dickinson, 139
Dinsdale, P.S., 171
Doggett, William H., 171, 172
Donahue, John, 21
Dowling, Hugh, 20
Draper Corp., 61
DuBois, ____, 88
Dudley, ____, 9
Durant, 131, 138
Eastman Gardner Company, 28
Edwards, O.F., 80
Elizabethtown, 139
Ellenburg, 139
Emoryville, 94
Empire State Forest Products Association, 147, 156, 175, 176
Emporium Forestry Company, 3, 11, 24, 32-35, 37, 38, 40, 45-54, 58, 60-66, 68, 69, 79, 80, 86, 87, 90, 91, 95, 98, 104-106, 111, 121, 124, 125, 142, 143, 145, 148, 156, 162, 165, 172, 173, 176
Emporium Lumber Company, 50, 51, 64, 87, 172
Essex County Republican, 141
Euba Mills, 139
Evans, J.F., 141
Evening Journal, The (Glens Falls), 141
Fernow, Bernard E., 160, 161, 166
Ferry, Hamilton, 72
Fields, A.J., 101
Finch-Pruyn and Company, 15, 21, 22, 26, 31, 71, 114, 170, 171
Fine, 141
Fish Creek, 20
Flanders, Arthur, 141
Forest and Stream, 158
Forest Commission (NYS), 128-130, 155, 156
Forest History Foundation, 174
Forestport, 113
Forest Preserve, 150, 159, 160

Forest Reserve, 128, 129
Fort Edward, 16
Fowler, George, 84
Fox, William, 6, 10, 79, 132-134, 142, 155, 156, 160
Frazer, ____, 111
Fulton, 1
Fulton Chain, 140
Galeton, Pa., 35, 37, 60, 64, 172
General Forestry Act, 129
Giddings, Charles, 135
Giedion, Siegfried, 27
Gilmour, J. D., 4, 45
Glens Falls, 1, 16, 20, 21, 170
Godey's Magazine, 4, 18, 158
Goodyear Lumber Company, 35
Gorman Brothers, 30
Goslin, E.B., 89
Gould Paper Company, 10, 20-22, 75
Grasse River Club, 49, 91
Grasse River Railroad, 47-51, 54-57, 60, 89, 111, 137, 143, 146, 169
Graves, Henry S., 161, 162
Greco, Frank, 47, 48
Greeley, Horace, 127
Hadley, F.H., 30
Hanlon, Howard, 156
Harper's Weekly, 3, 17, 84
Harrison, Benjamin, 166
Harrisville, 141
Harvard's School of Forestry, 172
Hawley, R.C., 172
Heltman, Helen, 63, 64
Heltman, Prof. H.J., 63, 64
Heywood-Wakefield Co., 50, 59, 62, 63
Hickey, 103
Higbey, Warren, 161
Higby, J.H., 141
Hill, C.L., 172
Hochschild, Harold, 5, 19, 20
Hollywood Club, 61
Holmes, George, 49
Holt Manufacturing Company, 11
Homelite Corp., 31
Hooper, Charles, 139
Hopkins, William, 135
Hopkinton, 141
Horse Shoe Station, 37
Hosley, Dr. Morrison, 114
Hough, Judge Franklin B., 159
Hudson Falls, 1, 16
Hudson River, 15, 16, 18, 21, 22
Hudson River Boom Association, 16
Hulse, James, 123, 124
Hyland, Dr., 113
Ice Cave Mountain, 11
Indian Lake, 22, 96, 140, 176
Indian River, 20
Industrial Workers of the World, 69
Inlet, 140
International Paper Co., 49, 83

Jackson, Harry, 79
Jennings, W.D., 140
Jessup, Morris K., 161
Jessup River, 22
Johnson, Harold, 126
Johnston and Son, 22, 83
Johnston and Strife, 83
Johnston, John E., 102
Jones Brook, 22
Jones, E.J., 64, 124
Jones, Joe, 88
Jones, Sherman, 95
Joy, Dr. E.H., 98
"Juvenal," 158
Kalm, Peter, 149
Kamp Kill Kare, 120, 123
Keating Summit, Pa., 35, 37, 50, 60
Keith, Herbert, 93
Kenwell, Wellington, 140
Kerr, Ed, 9
Kerr, Henry, 9
Ketzell, William, 88
Kildare, 67, 89, 136
Lafave, Henry, 122
Lafave, Mrs. Henry, 122
Lake Clear Junction, 171
Lake George, 149
Lake Placid, 9
Lake Ozonia, 72
Lanz, George, 110, 113
Laurentide Co., 146
LeClair, George, 95
Linn, ____, 11
Linn Tractor, 23
Lippencott's, 84
Litchfield Park, 83
Little Tupper Lake, 134, 156, 161
Logger's Handbook, 26, 27
Long Lake, 16, 96, 114, 140, 176
Loomis, Camp 134
Loon Lake, 139, 140
Low, A.A., 36, 37, 83
Lowrey, Dr. Paul H., 125
Lumber Camp News, The, 3, 16, 20, 25-31, 82, 85, 113, 114, 126
Lumber Mutual Casualty Insurance Co., 34, 106, 111, 112
Lyman, A.G., 35
Lyons Falls, 1, 21, 22,
M & M Railroad, 47
MacDonald, E.A., 18
MacDonald, George, 141
Maddox, Rev. Aaron, 26, 79, 82, 97, 98, 100
Marion River Carry, 120
Marleau, William, 92
Mason, Rev. Clarence W., 10, 97
Massawepie Club, 61
Maunder, Elwood R., 174, 175
McCarthy Bros., 83
McClinton, Margaret, 38

McCoy, George A. and Son, 35, 40, 41
McCulloch Motors Corp., 31
McKeever, 22
McKinney, George, 139
McLoughlin, William, 72
Meacham Lake, 83
Meader, George, 135
Meigs, Ferris J., 14, 18, 24, 70, 80, 85, 88, 94, 170
Mitchell, Billy, 93
Moody, Henry, 9
Moose River, 20-22
Moose River Lumber Co., 162
Morgan, J.P., 162
Morton, J. Sterling, 161
Mt. Arab, 138, 144
Murphy and Company, 10
Murray, W.H.H., 149
National Forest Commission, 161
National Progressive Party, 164
National Recovery Act, 174, 175
Nehasane, 83, 140
Nehasane Forestry Co., 83
Ne-Ha-Sa-Ne Park, 51, 161, 162, 164
Nehasane Park, 134
Nelson, Dr., 113
Newcomb, 1, 5, 20, 71, 83, 96, 114, 119, 166
Newman, 135
Newton Falls Paper Co., 49
New York & Ottawa Railroad, 130
New York Central Railroad, 54, 89, 130, 131, 141, 142
New York Civic League, 95
New York Forestry Association, 161
New York Lumber, 3
New York State College of Forestry, Cornell, 160, 166
New York State Department of Environmental Conservation, 176
New York State Forest Board, 150
New York School of Foresters, 168
New York Times, The, 120, 126
Nobleboro, 22
Noelk, Victor, 112
North Conifer, 121
North Creek, 176
Northeastern Logger, The, 85
North Elba, 134
Northern Logger, The, 85
Northern Logger and Timber Processor, The, 70, 84
Norwood, 170
Norwood Manufacturing Co., 26
O'Brien, William, 144
Old Forge, 140
Olmsteadville, 135
Onchiota, 139
Ord River, 20
Oswegatchie, 95, 141
Oval Wood Dish Corporation, 23, 67, 83
Owen, ____, 91
Owen, A.L., 64

Palmer, Atty. Gen. A. Mitchell, 69
Parrotte, Cpl. George, 102
Paul Smiths, 171
Paul Smiths' College, 166
Pettis, C.R., 144, 172
Piercefield, 47, 100, 118, 154
Pinchot, Gifford, 51, 158, 160-166, 169, 170, 172
Pioneer, 31
Plumadore Station, 134
Poland, 1
Portageville, 35
Port Kent, 135
Post Standard, The (Syracuse), 124, 126
Potsdam, 1
Potter Wood, 26
Prevost, Mrs. Joseph, 141
Pullman Mill, 110, 113
Ranger School, 166, 167, 171, 171
Raquette Lake, 16, 123
Raquette Lake Railway, 131
Raquette Pond, 22
Raquette River, 16, 18, 20, 22, 25, 103
Raquette River Paper Co., 26, 49, 67
Recknagel, Prof. A.B., 66, 130, 145, 171-175
Reds, 69
Reed, Rev. Frank, 27, 82, 92, 93, 97, 101, 113
Reynoldston, 139
Rich Lumber Co., 93, 167
Riley, John, 91
Rix, Julian, 151
Roberts, J.E., 140
Rockefeller, William, 162
Roosevelt, Franklin D., 174
Roosevelt, Teddy, 161, 164
Rothrock, J.T., 161
Round Island, Pa., 34
Rowe, C.W., 135
Ruskin, John, 150
Sadley, Charles, 56
St. Elizabeth's Hospital, 113, 123
St. Paul's Roman Catholic Church, 100
St. Regis Falls, 94, 139
St. Regis Paper Company, 22, 50, 96
Salmon River, 15
Samson, Nelson T., 4, 69, 83
Santa Clara Lumber Company, 14, 18, 24, 26, 70, 85, 94, 170, 171
Saranac & Lake Placid Railroad, 130, 131
Saranac Lake, 114, 130
Saranac River, 156
Schroon Lake, 17
Scribner's, 84
Senftner, Dr., 120-122
Shove, Ben, 64
Simmons, Fred, 26, 29
Sisson and White, 83
Sisson, Charles, 68
Sissonville, 25
Skenesborough, 15
Skiff, A.M., 139

Slade Tractor Company, 30
Smith, Fremont, 139
Smith, Gov. Al, 106
Smith, Jesse, 96
Smith, Perkins, 139
Smith, William, 21
Society of American Foresters, 167, 176
South Conifer, 121
South Meadows, 9, 135
Sovic, Larry, 64
Spafford, 155
Spear, Joe, 91
Springs, Gilbert, 30
Stanyon, Frank, 140
State College of Forestry, Syracuse University, 166
State Industrial Commission, 106, 111
Stewart, A.C., 49
Stock, John, 46, 101
Stoddard, Seneca Ray, 152, 153
Stony Creek, 20
Sugar Trust, 165
Sullivan, James, 67
Sykes, Chester, 64
Sykes, Frank, 11
Sykes, George W., 5, 33, 50, 52, 60, 62, 64, 112, 156
Sykes, Roy O., 33, 64
Sykes, Stella Walker, 40
Sykes, W. Clyde, 3, 33, 46, 51, 60, 64, 69, 88, 91, 94-96, 98, 101, 102, 120-122, 124-126, 142, 144, 145, 147, 165, 171, 175
Sykes, William Lowther (W.L.), 5, 32-34, 37-41, 47-49, 62, 63, 68, 91, 94, 99, 104-106, 143, 144, 146, 147, 166, 169, 171, 173, 176, 177
Syracuse University, 34
Taylor, F.W., 85
Tebo, 103, 104
Thendara, 110
Ticonderoga, 83
Todd, J.B., 11
Travelers, The, 106
Troy Record, The, 141
Truman, Alfred, 46, 86-88, 90, 101, 120
Tug Hill, 102
Tupper Lake Herald, 47, 124-126
Tupper Lake (village), 1, 22, 40, 88, 91, 93, 95, 96, 141, 165
Tupper Lake Junction, 61, 170
Turner, ____, 83
Turner, William, 91
Twin Pond, 141
United Labor Agency, 68
Upper Saranac Lake, 167
Usher mills, 26
Utica, 113
Utowanna Lake, 16
Vance, Lee J., 4, 18
Vanderbilt, George W., 160
Wade, Charles S., 30
Wainwright Commission, 106

Walsh, James, 91
Wanakena, 166-168
Warrensburg, 20, 152, 166
Watertown, 1
Watertown Daily Standard, 94
Watertown Daily Times, 124, 126
Webb, Dr.W. Seward, 51, 131, 138, 160, 162, 165, 170
Wells, 140
West Canada Creek, 22
Weston, W.M., 37

Westport, 139
White, Stewart Edward, 85
Whitehall, 15
Whitney, C.L., 160
Whitney Park, 83
Whitney, William C., 51, 138, 162, 165, 170
Williams, Harry, 120
Wilson, Ellwood, 146, 147
Winthrop, 101
Woodsmen's Field Day, 30, 31
Workmen's Compensation Act, 106
Yale Forestry School, 172